Sulzer Types 2 and 3

BR LOCOMOTIVES:2

Sulzer Types 2 and 3

A.T.H. Tayler

LONDON

IAN ALLAN LTD

First published 1984

ISBN 0 7110 1340 3

© Ian Allan Ltd 1984

Published by Ian Allan Ltd, Shepperton, Surrey;
and printed by Ian Allan Printing Ltd at their works
at Coombelands in Runnymede, England.

Contents

Left: Nos D6594 and D6596 pass Wilton South with the 08.50 Brighton-Exeter on 7 September 1968. The leading locomotive is one of 12 built with a reduced profile for working the Hastings line. *G. F. Gillham*

Cover: Class 26 No 26.034 climbs away from Insch with the 15.47 Aberdeen-Inverness in April 1982. *R. T. Nunn*

Preface

The British Railways Type 2s and their Type 3 derivatives with Sulzer in-line engines ultimately totalled 692 locomotives. The Type 2s were products of the original 'Pilot Scheme' of the late 1950s and in expanding the two original batches, each of 20 locomotives, from BR Derby with British Thompson-Houston equipment and the Birmingham Railway Carriage & Wagon Company with Crompton Parkinson equipment, batches differed as experience and new developments evolved.

This account seeks to show the background to the original concepts and to highlight the Technical features of these essentially low-medium power general purpose locomotives. In the 20-odd years since the appearance of the initial locomotives, operating requirements have changed quite radically. With the disappearance of many of the rural feeder lines, with electrification and with the complete change in freight policy, much of the traffic for which the lower-medium powered general purpose loco-

motives were intended has disappeared and this has led to heavy reductions in that type of motive power and standardisation on types which have equipment with the widest use throughout British Railways. By the time this account appears in print much of what is said will be history and it is hoped that this book keeps alive the memory of the Class 24 and 25 locomotives as well as giving an account of the Class 26, 27 and 33 locomotives.

In the preparation of this book I would like to thank the many friends and colleagues who have provided information and suggestions. In particular I would like to thank my former colleagues in Sulzer and the various Regions of British Rail. Thanks must also go to Joan Thomas who did the typing and who spent many hours setting out much of the data in the original manuscript.

Class 27 No 27.014 receives attention at Eastfield depot on 13 August 1983. *J. C. Hillmer*

1 Origin and Development

The British Railway Modernisation plan announced on 25 January 1955 is generally considered to be the turning point in the change from steam motive power to diesel and electric. The Transport Act of 1953 was formulated at a time when it was felt the nation demanded change and one change was to be the modernisation of motive power in a bid to reduce operating costs. The main financial benefit was considered to be obtainable by a rapid replacement of steam by diesel traction: electrification had obvious advantages but would take a far longer time to generate increased net revenue.

A policy was formulated to institute a three-year trial period for the new diesel locomotive types which had been recommended and on 16 October 1955 an announcement was made advising that a pilot scheme for a total of 171 main line diesel locomotives (later modified to 174) had been approved covering three classes of duty as follows:

Freight	Type A	800-1,000hp
Mixed Traffic	Type B	1,000-1,250hp
Heavy Duty	Type C	2,000hp and over

When the 1956 locomotive building programme was published at the end of 1955 it was confirmed that orders had been placed for 171 locomotives which would carry out pilot trials before a major change-over to diesel traction, estimated then to require some 2,500 units. Deliveries could commence in 18 months to two years from a variety of manufacturers, summarised below in Table 1.

So the Sulzer-engined mixed traffic locomotives were initiated, laying the foundation for a total of 594 generally similar locomotives later to be known as Type 2 and subsequently better identified by classification as Classes 24, 25, 26 and 27.

A rather loose specification was issued to the various contenders for the 'pilot scheme' locomotives

Table 1

Freight (800-1,000hp) — Type A

No	Type	Horsepower	Builder	Engine	Transmission	Region
20	Bo-Bo	1,000	EE/VF	EE	EE	LM
10	Bo-Bo	800	NBL	Paxman	BT-H	LM
10	Bo-Bo	800	Derby	Paxman	GEC	E

Mixed Traffic (1,000-1,250hp) — Type B

No	Type	Horsepower	Builder	Engine	Transmission	Region
10	Bo-Bo	1,100	EE/VF	Napier	EE	E
20	Bo-Bo	1,160	BRCW	Sulzer	CP	E
20	A1A-A1A	1,250	Brush	Mirrless	Brush	E
10	Bo-Bo	1,000	NBL	MAN	GEC	E
6	Bo-Bo	1,000	NBL	MAN	Voith	W
20	Co-Bo	1,200	MV	Crossley	MV	LM
20	Bo-Bo	1,160	Derby	Sulzer	BT-H	LM

Heavy Duty (2,000hp and over) — Type C

No	Type	Horsepower	Builder	Engine	Transmission	Region
10	1Co-Co1	2,000	EE/VF	EE	EE	E
5	A1A-A1A	2,000	NBL	MAN	Voith	W
10	1Co-Co1	2,300	Derby	Sulzer	CP	LM

Shortly after it was announced a further three locomotives were added as follows:

No	Type	Horsepower	Builder	Engine	Transmission	Region
3	B-B	2,000	Swindon MMB	Mekydro		W

to encourge the development of individual ideas within a fairly broad spectrum. It was envisaged that locomotives in the 'Type B' range would handle the same type of traffic as steam locomotives in the '4MT' category and this would include suburban services in and around the major cities and railway centres. While some modernisation of steam motive power for such services was taking place, there were still many services in the hands of rather small and ageing tank engines which were becoming expensive and difficult to maintain to the necessary standards.

The basis of the British Railway dieselisation scheme policy had been recommended by the responsible engineers who were anxious to use the experience so gained to develop sound future standard locomotives, but the commercial and operating people were quick to see the advantages to be obtained from the early elimination of steam and its replacement by a more modern image. The trial period was abruptly abandoned and further orders were placed before any of the initial orders had been completed. E. S. Cox covers this particular aspect in his own published account of the period of change and the following extract from Volume 2 of his *Locomotive Panorama* puts the matter in perspective:

'If these orders had been followed by the three-year moratorium which was at that time agreed, we might not have learned all about the inherent characteristics of this or that product since we now know that it can take as long as five years and even more before one really knows what can happen to any given engine or transmission in rail service. On the other hand there would have been time to consolidate preferred training, maintenance and trouble-shooting organisation and equipment and we would have been in a good position to write the definitive specifications for further advance into dieselisation.

'Instead there now followed several years of confused council, the outcome of which was the decision to go ahead with bulk purchase, not only of some of the types represented within the initial 174, but of other new types also, straight from the drawing board. Worse still these new measures did not even await the delivery of the whole 174.'

Be that as it may, the first orders for Type B locomotives with Sulzer engines were placed at the end of 1955; 20 on Derby Works and 20 on the Birmingham Railway Carriage, Wagon & Finance Company (BRCW) of Smethwick to a general specification which laid down a maximum axle load of 18.75tons, a maximum operating speed of 75mph and provision of steam train-heating equipment. Braking of the locomotive was to be by an approved straight-air system but train braking was to be vacuum. Particular attention was to be paid to appearance and while the paint colours were specified (Brunswick Green for the main body parts) additional embellishments were left to individual builders. Ability to run two or more loco-

motives coupled under the control of one crew (multiple-unit working) was a requirement and where steam heating equipment was fitted, standard gangway communication between locomotives was to be provided. British Railways standard details were to be incorporated in the mechanical parts in certain instances — coupling and drawgear, of course — and the whole was to be within the British Railway C1 loading gauge.

In order that Regional requirements should not be ignored, Regional Design Offices were appointed to liaise with the locomotive builders and the principle adopted was that the Region to which a particular type of locomotive was to be allocated should act as the 'Parent Design Office'. Thus the Derby-built locomotives initially allocated to the London Midland Region were the responsibility of the Derby Design Office, who in this case were also the mechanical parts designers and main contractors, while the locomotives ordered on BRCW were the responsibility of the Eastern Region Design Office at Doncaster. It was, in essence, a tripartite arrangement because the contractor exerted considerable influence and provided advice on installation and other aspects affecting the design.

Until the decision to change from steam to diesel and electric traction there had been only limited experience with diesel locomotives on British Railways. At the time of nationalisation the largest user of diesel shunting locomotives had been the LMSR, while small numbers were in use, or on order, by the other three railways. The LMS had just completed one 1,600hp Co-Co locomotive, No 10000 and the second was well advanced and two others, No 10100 the 2,000hp 2D2 'Fell' diesel-mechanical and No 10800, an 833hp Bo-Bo diesel-electric, were on order. The Southern Railway had on order three high-speed 1Co-Co1 units of 1,750hp but work had not proceeded beyond the drawing board, the first — No 10201, not being completed until late 1950. There were however considerable developments overseas and by the late 1950s a large number of successful and reliable general purpose locomotives had been produced on four axles and with either single or double cabs.

As long ago as 1939 the Swiss Federal Railways had purchased two 1,200hp Bo-Bo diesel-electric locomotives for secondary lines. These were of light-weight construction and weighed only 65 tonnes with a maximum service speed of 68mph. They incorporated Sulzer medium-speed eight-cylinder in-line engines, forerunners of the postwar LDA28 type which, by 1955, had been developed and modernised to produce 1,160hp in the six-cylinder in-line version.

For the BR Type B range the choice of engine lay between six-cylinder in-line, eight- and 12-cylinder Vee medium speed engines and 12-cylinder quick-running engines. Compared to many overseas railways already operating diesel locomotives, BR had the problem of a restrictive loading gauge and one might

Swiss Federal Railways Bm 4/4 No 18451 (ex 1001) on train from Singen at Etzwilen in May 1964. *A. T. H. Tayler*

have expected a trend towards quick running, light-weight engines, but the natural conservatism of railway engineers, coupled with the known experience of the USA, pointed towards the slower, heavier and more rugged medium speed engines. Experience in the USA and elsewhere clearly pointed towards maintenance costs being proportional to the number of parts requiring to be dismantled and re-erected, almost irrespective of size and even the limited experience in the UK with No 10000/1 and Nos 10201-3 showed an advantage compared to the quick-running engines in Nos 10100, 10800 and 11001. Nevertheless as Table 1 indicates there were representatives from both camps although the medium speed engines accounted for a little over 75% of the total.

We are concerned here with the Sulzer engines only and the 20 locomotives each of Derby and BRCW design and their derivatives. As already intimated, increases in orders over and above the initial 20 of each type began before the prototypes were in service and by the middle of 1957 Derby Works had received an order for an additional 10 locomotives for the Eastern Region with BRCW receiving an order for another 18 for the Scottish Region. At this time the Southern Region was looking for approximately 100 diesel locomotives to supplement the electric locomotives and multiple-unit stock for the Kent Coast electrification. Although the Region had been pro-

mised the loan of 15 from the LMR allocation, special operating considerations clearly showed a need for Bo-Bo locomotives of a power somewhere between Types B and C with a special requirement for electric train-heating, because the Region did not intend to keep and maintain a very small number of steam-heated passenger vehicles for a limited number of services, the more so since its electric locomotives would not provide steam heating. There were other requirements which will be mentioned later.

Because of the obvious power gap between Types B and C of 750hp and because there was a clearly identified need for locomotives in that range, the BR specification was altered to include a Type D mixed traffic range of 1,500-1,750hp. Then in August 1957 the whole range of locomotives was redesignated as follows:

Class	Horsepower	Running numbers
1	750-1,000	D8000-8999
2	1,000-1,250	D5000-6499
3	1,500-1,750	D6500-7999
4	2,000-2,500	D1-999
5	3,000 and over	D1000-1999 D9000-9999

In December 1957 an order was placed with BRCW for 45 Class 3 Bo-Bo locomotives of 1,550hp, numbered D6500-44, the first to be in service by the end of 1959. The mechanical parts would be based on the BRCW Type 2 then under construction but modified to take an eight-cylinder in-line Sulzer engine. In June

9

Official photo of No D5000 after completion at Derby in 1958. *BR*

1958 orders were placed for a further 84 Type 2 locomotives to be built by BR Workshops making the total on order 114. The Eastern Region would take 66 and the remaining 18 would go to the then operationally separate North Eastern Region. Because of the delay in producing the new Type 3 for the Southern Region, 15 Type 2s from the first build, originally destined for the London Midland Region, would be loaned to the Southern Region to enable some steam workings to be eliminated, initially in the Faversham-Dover area.

By the middle of 1958 some patterns were emerging, the chief of which was the intention of the Eastern Region to eliminate steam working from East Anglia and its London suburban services, hence the intended allocation of more locomotives to that Region.

The first Derby-built Type 2 No D5000 emerged in July 1958 and was presented at Marylebone station on 24 July for inspection by the Chairman of the British Transport Commission, Gen Sir Brian Robertson.

The first of the BRCW Type 2s, No D5300, was completed in September 1958 and was delivered to Doncaster where it underwent inspection and acceptance test runs prior to delivery to Hornsey depot of the Eastern Region, following which it was stated it and others of its class would replace 'N2' 0-6-2T locomotives and others on the suburban services to Hitchin and Hertford.

Meanwhile No D5000, after working special test trips with 15 empty coaches weighing some 460tons between Chaddesden sidings, Derby and Liverpool via Cheadle Junction and Allerton Junction, commenced working between Derby and Manchester and Liverpool Central on service trains to train drivers. Nos D5300/1, when accepted, carried out crew training on service trains between King's Cross and Hertford North or King's Cross and Welwyn.

By the end of 1958 main line diesel orders were gathering magnitude and totalled 655 — all except the 22 'Deltics' and the 65 BRCW Type 3s being extensions of the 14 different types included in the original pilot scheme plans. The Derby Type 2s had reached a total order of 114, the BRCW Type 2s had expanded to 38 and the BRCW Type 3s to 65.

By now the number of Derby Type 2s had exceeded Derby Works capability and in the 1959 building programme the works and Regional allocations were as follows:

Type	Builder	Number	Numbers	Region
2	Derby	20	D5000-20	LM
	Derby	10	D5021-30	E
	Crewe	36	D5030-65	E
	Derby	10	D5066-75	E
	Crewe	18	D5076-93	E
	Darlington	2	D5094/5	E
	Darlington	18	D5096-113	NE
2	BRCW	20	D5300-19	E
	BRCW	9	D5320-28	E
	BRCW	18	D5329-46	Sc

In April 1959 the BR Type 2 was further extended to 151 by an order for a further 37, all to be built at Derby.

One feature of both the early BR-built and BRCW Type 2 was their failure to achieve the design weight, for although the official description of the Derby-built locomotives declared the weight at 75 tons, No D5000, when weighed, tipped the scales at 79ton 6cwt, by which time too many of the first batch were under construction to achieve any worthwhile changes to bring the weight down other than by omitting boilers and running with empty tanks. The BRCW locomotives, while over their designed weight, came out at 77ton 17cwt and were declared as such.

Resulting from the increase in weight of the BR Type 2 was an unexpected restriction imposed by the Southern Region Civil Engineer on route availability on the South Eastern and Central Divisions, one of which

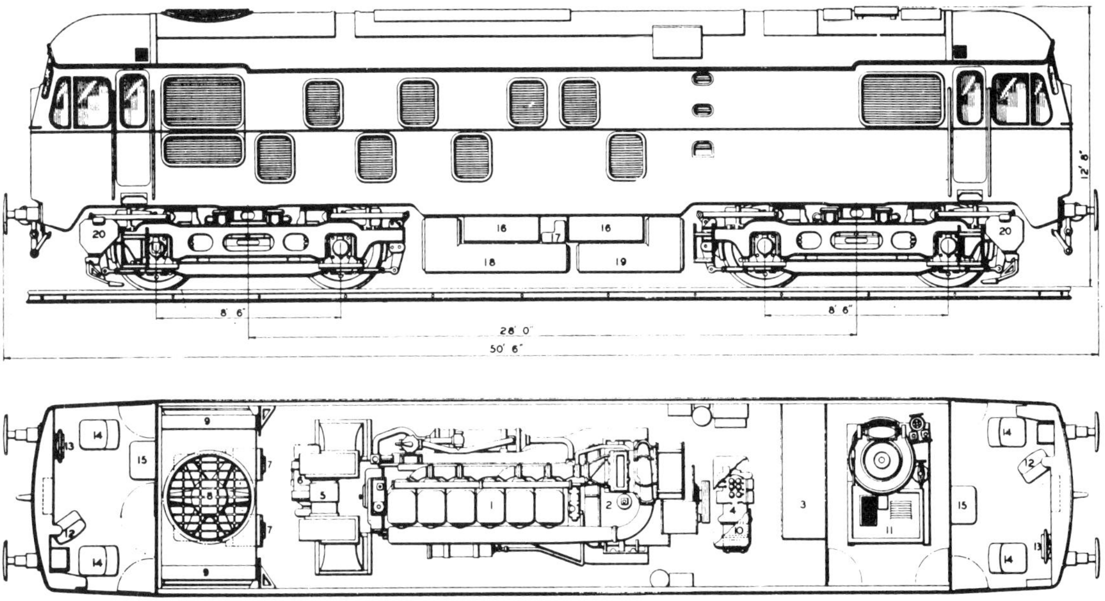

General arrangement of British Railways Type 2 locomotive built in Derby workshops.
Indicated components are :

1, Sulzer engine ; 2, B.T.H. generator ; 3, control cubicle ; 4, compressor ; 5, blower set ; 6, fuel, oil and water pumps ;
7, exhauster ; 8, radiator fan and motor ; 9, radiator ; 10, brake gear cubicle ; 11, Stone-Vapor train-heating boiler ;
12, driver's controller ; 13, hand brake ; 14, seat ; 15, clothes locker and cooker ; 16, battery box ; 17, drain tank ;
18, fuel tank ; 19, water tank ; 20, sand box.

Fig 1   Arrangement drawing of No D5000

was the complete ban on working coupled to each other or to any other locomotive except for certain short trips from stations to motive power depots.

After delivery of the first few units it became apparent that the speed ceiling of 75mph was unduly restrictive, added to which provision of a little more power would be advantageous. In the course of normal development the power output of the Sulzer six-cylinder engine had been increased to give a continuous traction output of 1,250bhp at 750rpm by the introduction of charge air cooling, details of which are given later.

The operating convenience of motive power which did not require frequent visits to depots was immediately apparent and pressure to press forward with dieselisation of many areas resulted in further orders. Specifications were hastily altered to take account of the limited experience already obtained and to introduce features to permit easier operation; eg all diesel-electric locomotives subsequent to the 'pilot' orders were to be capable of multiple-unit

Class 26 — official photo.   *BR*

No D5240 showing change of style and two-tone green.
Morgan-Wells

working with each other and the system originally introduced on the English Electric and Sulzer-engined locomotives was adopted. This involved the fitting of English Electric 27-way couplers on the bufferbeams and the provision between the locomotives of an air line fed from the leading driver's controller for the control of engine speed.

Further Type 2 locomotives were ordered from both BR and BRCW and by May 1960 another 25 to BR design had been ordered from Darlington Works; although initially noted as of 1,160hp, this was later altered to 1,250hp. While these 25 still had BT-H electrical equipment, the company had combined with Metropolitan-Vickers to become the Associate Electrical Industries and all future reference will be to AEI. Meanwhile BRCW had received orders for 69 more of its Type 2, but the electrical contractor had been changed to GEC, Whitton. Again the engine was up-rated to 1,250bhp at 750rpm and there were some detail changes. The total now on order or in course of delivery from BRCW was 116.

In order to distinguish it from the earlier Sulzer 6LDA28-A engine, the latest version was designated 6LDA28-B, the same engine being used in the BR and BRCW designs of locomotive, but with different main and auxiliary generators so that complete power units were not interchangeable.

Now the pattern had been established and although no more Type 2s were ordered from BRCW because the company closed down after delivery of the last, No D5315 in September 1962, the BR design was adopted as a BR standard. Totals were 151 with 1,160hp engines and 327 with 1,250hp engines. There were five variants of the former and eight

variants of the latter, some of them fairly minor, the most obvious being the changes in body design from D5233 onwards following the elimination of gangway doors in the cab fronts.

The BRCW Type 3 is included in this survey because it was a development of the original BRCW Type 2. As already mentioned, the Southern Region had a particular need for a locomotive rather more powerful and versatile than the Type 2 and for the first time produced a performance specification. There were a number of prime requirements, viz:

● Haulage of 700ton freight trains on ruling gradient of 1 in 70.
● Haulage of 375ton passenger and van trains over electrified and non-electrified lines.
● Capability of heating such trains electrically.
● Haulage of electric multiple-unit stock at normal service speed over all routes in emergency.
● Maximum service speed of 85mph.
● Working of vacuum and air-braked rolling stock.
● A wide route availability.

A Bo-Bo locomotive was preferred on the grounds of weight and cost and Regional investigations had shown that the necessary power, estimated at around 1,600hp gross, could be provided within a locomotive similar to either the BR or BRCW Type 2. On the other hand the BTC had produced the Type D specification covering the 1,500-1,750hp range and had decided on 80mph as a reasonable top speed for the class. Eventually two practical alternatives emerged, a 1,750hp 105ton Co-Co, put forward by English Electric, with a 12-cylinder Vee engine; and a 76ton-Bo-Bo, put forward by BRCW, with an eight-cylinder in-line Sulzer engine.

Of the two, the BTC was pushing the Co-Co, as the

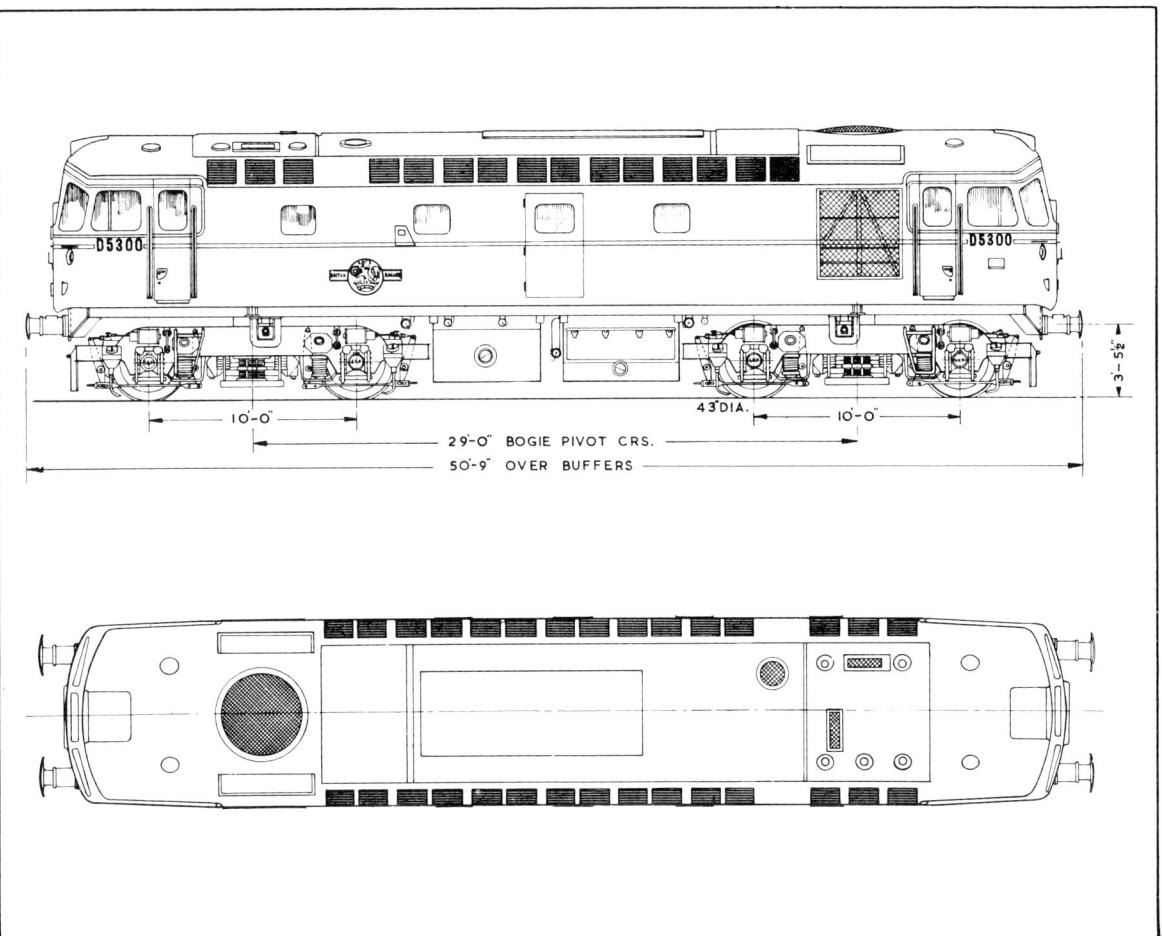

Fig 2 Arrangement drawing of No D5300

committee wanted to make this a standard BR design (in the event it emerged as the Class 37) but it did not conform to requirements in two important respects: it could not provide electric train-heating and it did not have air train-braking equipment. Also, when asked for a provisional route-availability, the Civil Engineer gave the Bo-Bo almost universal acceptance but the Co-Co was barred from several important routes.

In the end agreement was reached on most of the important aspects of the design but the BTC held out against a top speed higher than 80mph and after some considerable argument agreed to the provision of the slightly more expensive but infinitely more versatile combined Auto-air/vacuum train-braking equipment — a difficult decision for the BTC as it had only recently decided to retain the vacuum brake, except for electric multiple-unit stock! The same braking system was also employed on the 24 Bo-Bo electric locomotives built at Doncaster (Nos E5000-5023), later E5001-24 and subsequently Classes 71 and 74). With the need to work locomotive-hauled van and freight trains over the Tunbridge Wells-Hastings

route, it would have been desirable to build all of the Type 3s to that loading gauge, but it was estimated the additional design work would delay deliveries of the first 45 desperately needed to eliminate steam by the inception Phase 2 of the Kent Coast electrification and the idea was dropped.

The design proceeded on the basis of mechanical parts similar to the BRCW 1,160hp Type 2 but with two important differences: no nose end gangways were required and a much neater front end with the standard Southern Region two-character roller blind route indicator incorporating letters as well as numbers resulted. Bogies generally similar to the earlier Type 2 were provided but the secondary spring-ing was modified to incorporate coil springs and hydraulic dampers in place of the transverse laminated springs of the original Type 2 design.

As previously mentioned, an order was placed on BRCW for an initial 45 locomotives in December 1957, the parent design office being that of the Region's Electrical Engineer at London Bridge who handled the main contract for the mechanical parts assisted by the CM&EE's Technical Office at Brighton.

A further 20 Type 3s were ordered in October

No D6500 — official photograph. *BR*

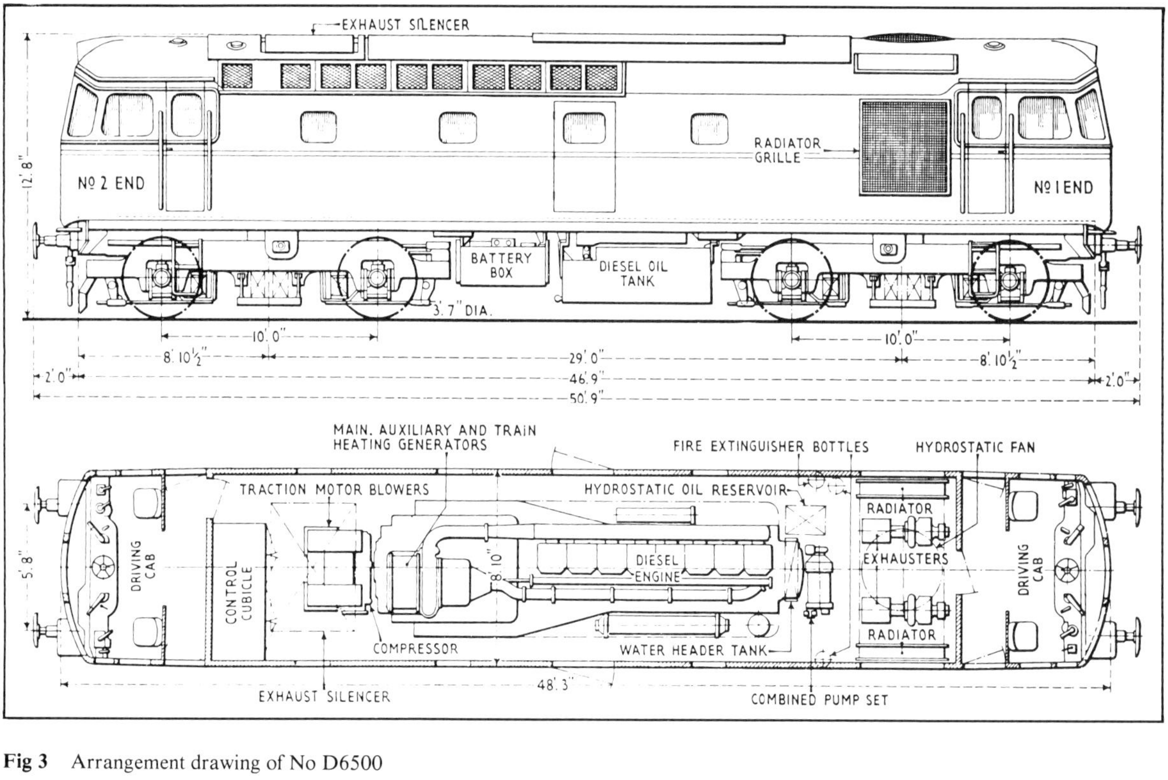

Fig 3   Arrangement drawing of No D6500

1958, sufficient to cover, with the Bo-Bo electric loco-motives, the requirements of the Kent Coast scheme. Further locomotives would be needed to eliminate steam completely from all lines in Kent and Sussex and now it was important to cover the Tunbridge Wells-Hastings line. In July 1959 12 narrow-bodied versions of the Type 3 were ordered and by May 1960 orders had been placed with BRCW for a final batch of 21 'standard' Type 3s, making a grand total of 98. By comparision with the Eastern Region, which would have four completely different makes of Type 2, the Southern would be highly standardised, having achieved this end by having perhaps more ability than others to make up its mind aided by its basically electric traction background.

The first Type 3 was completed in December 1959, practically to programme, and was delivered to the Southern Region on 17 December 1959, although not officially taken into stock until January 1960. Num-bered D6500 and painted in generally the same style as the BRCW Type 2s, it was allocated to Hither Green MPD. Unlike its earlier cousins, and due to the extreme

Leading particulars of BR Classes 24, 25, 26 and 27 locomotives

	Class 24	Class 25	Class 26	Class 27
Builder	BR Derby	BR and BP[1]	BRCW	BRCW
Engine (Sulzer)	6LDA28-A	6LDA28-B	6LDA28-A	6LDA28-B
Electrical equipment	BT-H	AEI[2]	CP	GEC[3]
Wheel arrangement	Bo-Bo	Bo-Bo	Bo-Bo	Bo-Bo
Weight in working order (ton-cwt)	71-0 to 79-16	70-5 to 74-8	73-6 to 77-17	71-4 to 73-6
Maximum axle load (ton-cwt)	18-0 to 19-19	18-0 to 18-17	18-8 to 18-12	17-18 to 18-8
Adhesion weight (ton-cwt)[4]	71-0 to 79-16	70-5 to 74-8	73-6 to 77-17	71-4 to 73-6
Maximum speed (mph)	75	90	80	90
Maximum tractive effort (lb)	40,000	39,000 (25 only) 45,000	42,000	42,000
Continuous rated tractive effort (lb)	21,300 at 14.8mph	20,800 at 17.1mph	30,000 at 11.25mph	25,000 at 14.0mph
Engine (bhp)	1,160 at 750rpm	1,250 at 750rpm	1,160 at 750rpm	1,250 at 750rpm
Length over buffers (ft-in)	50-6	50-6	50-9	50-9
Overall width inc handrails (ft-in)	9-1	9-1	9-3	9-3
Width over body (ft-in)	8-10	8-10	8-10	8-10
Overall height (ft-in)	12-8	12-8	12-8	12-8
Wheel diameter (new) (ft-in)	3-9	3-9	3-7	3-7
Bogie Centres (ft-in)	28-0	28-0	29-0	29-0
Bogie wheelbase (ft-in)	8-6	8-6	10-0	10-0
Total wheelbase (ft-in)	36-6	36-6	39-0	39-0
Minimum radius curve (chains)	$4\frac{1}{2}$	$4\frac{1}{2}$	$4\frac{1}{2}$	$4\frac{1}{2}$
Fuel capacity incl boiler (gal)	630	620	600	600
Water capacity (gal)[5]	450/600	580	550	450
Main generator type	RTB15656	RTB15656	CG391A1	WT981
Traction motor type	137BY	137BX (25 only) 253AY	C171A1 (20 only) C171D3	WT459
Building dates	1958-61	1961-67	1958-59	1961-63

Notes:
1 Built at Darlington, Derby and Crewe BR and Gorton-Beyer, Peacock.
2 Associated Electrical Industries — merger of BT-H and MV (now GEC).
3 GEC Whitton, now part of GEC (EEC+MV+BT-H+GEC Whitton)
4 Varies between limits shown in different builds.
5 Where boilers are fitted.

Left: **Unidentified Type 2 arriving at Dalmally, August 1969.** *D. Birch*

Right: **No D6577 pilots No 34023** Blackmore Vale **through Medstead and Four Marks, 18 September 1966.** *J. Scrace*

care taken by both BRCW and the Region, it weighed 73.4tons — nearly two tons below the original estimate.

Following clearance tests in July 1960 the Civil Engineer gave the standard Type 3s almost universal acceptance over the Southern Region, only the Hastings line being barred, together with seven minor branch lines. Thirty-eight locomotives were taken into stock in 1960, 41 in 1961 and the order was completed by May 1962.

Leading particulars of BR Class 33

	Class 33	Class 33/1	Class 33/2
Builder	BRCW	BRCW	BRCW
Engine (Sulzer)	8LDA28-A	8LDA28-A	8LDA28-A
Electrical equipment	CP	CP	CP
Wheel arrangement	Bo-Bo	Bo-Bo	Bo-Bo
Weight in working order (ton-cwt)	73-8	77-6	74-4
Maximum axle load (ton-cwt)	18-10	19-8	18-11
Adhesion weight (ton-cwt)	73-8	77-6	74-4
Maximum speed (mph)	85	85	85
Minimum tractive effort (lb)	45,000	45,000	45,000
Continuous rated tractive effort (lb)	26,000 at 17.5mph	26,000 at 17.5mph	26,000 at 17.5mph
Engine output (bhp)	1,550	1,550	1,550
Length over buffers (ft-in)	50-9	50-9	50-9
Overall width inc handrails (ft-in)	9-3	8-8 footsteps, 8-5$\frac{5}{16}$	9-3
Width over body (ft-in)	8-10	8-1$\frac{1}{4}$	8-10
Overall height (ft-in)	12-8	12-8	12-8
Wheel diameter (new) (ft-in)	3-7	3-7	3-7
Bogie centres (ft-in)	29-0	29-0	29-0
Bogie wheelbase (ft-in)	10-0	10-0	10-0
Total wheelbase (ft-in)	39-0	39-0	39-0
Minimum radius curve[1] (chains)	4	4	4
Fuel capacity (gal)	800	800	800
Main generator type	CG391B1	CG391B1	CG391B1
Heating generator type[2]	CAG392A1	CAG392A1	CAG392A1
Traction motor type	C171C2	C171C2	C171C2
Building dates	1960-62	modified 1966/67[3]	1962

Notes:
1 Can negotiate 3$\frac{1}{3}$ chains with $\frac{3}{4}$in gauge widening.
2 Combined in same frame as main generator, output up to 235kW at 750V.
3 Original build 1960-62, 19 locomotives only.

2 The Power Equipment

Let us now look at the technical specifications of the original British Railways and BRCW batches of 20 each. Details of the two builds are given in Table 2 below and the general arrangement drawings Figs 1 and 2.

As can be seen from the general arrangement diagrams, the design approaches differed somewhat as far as bogies and bodies were concerned and while the BRCW locomotive employed glass reinforced plastics for cab roof ends and some roof sections, the

Table 2

	British Railways Type 2 (Class 24)	**BRCW Type 2 (Class 26)**
Type of engine	6LDA28-A	6LDA28-A
	4-stroke turbocharged	4-stroke turbocharged
Nominal output (bhp)	1,160	1,160
Wheel diameter (ft-in)	3-9	3-7
Bogie wheelbase (ft-in)	8-6	10-0
Total wheelbase (ft-in)	36-6	39-0
Overall length (ft-in)	50-6	50-9
Overall height from rail level (ft-in)	12-8	12-8
Minimum clearance above rail level (in)	6	6
Transmission equipment		
Main generator, rigidly coupled to crankshaft	British Thompson-Houston Type RTB15656	Crompton Parkinson CG391A1
Excitation	Differential exciter	Series, shunt and separate
Continuous rating	1,400A 515V	1,720A 440V
One-hour rating	1,500A 480V	1,925A 393V
Traction Motors		
Number	4	4
Connections	All in parallel	All in parallel
Type	British Thompson-Houston 137BY	Crompton Parkinson C171A1
	Nose suspended	Nose suspended
	Force ventilated	Force ventilated
Ratings V	525	440
A	350	430
Speed (rpm)	561	337
Locomotive ratings		
Tractive effort (lb) (max)	40,000	42,000
(cont)	21,300 at 14.8mph	30,000 at 11.25mph
Miscellaneous details		
Maximum speed (mph)	75mph	80mph
Weight in working order (ton-cwt)	79-16	77-17
Minimum radius curve (chains)	$4\frac{1}{2}$	$4\frac{1}{2}$
Fuel tank capacity (gal)	630	Engine 500
		Boiler 100
Engine starting battery	155 Ahrs 72 cells NiFe DL15	Nickel-Cadmium type

Top: **Bogie of BR Type 2.** *BR*

Above: **No D5011 at Gillingham — Athermos axleboxes.**
A. T. H. Tayler

Derby design employed a mixed steel and aluminium construction.

Both designs employed bodies of the 'bridge' type based on the Warren girder principle with integral underframe and bodysides. This shows up more clearly in the British Railways design because of the positions of the body-side mounted air intakes disposed so as to miss the main frame members. The BRCW design on the other hand has the air intakes above the cant rail in the small curvature of the roof profile leaving space for small windows, four in all, on either side of the equipment compartment.

In both cases bogies of the swing bolster, modified Pennsylvania type are employed, but there the similarity ends. The British Railways design is a combined riveted/fabricated structure with girder-type side frames outside the primary and secondary coil springs which does not exactly make for good accessibility. Axleboxes are connected by underslung equalisers on which the primary springs rest. While roller bearing axleboxes were employed generally, 10 locomotives were equipped with Athermos plain bearing axleboxes

in which a positive oil feed is provided by an integral oil thrower always ensuring a plentiful supply of oil to the bearing.

BRCW favoured fabricated steel box-section bogie side frames which also housed the equalising beams, placed on top of the axleboxes. In the initial batch of 20, transverse laminated secondary springs were employed. Body load and traction forces were taken through a deep, large diameter, centre casting carried by the swing bolster and the traction forces thence to the bogie frame by manganese steel friction pads.

In both cases, conventional axlebox guides were provided with renewable wearing surfaces. These gave a measure of damping for the coil secondary springs of the Derby design bogie.

In both designs conventional clasp brakes with cast iron blocks were fitted, operated by bogie-mounted compressed air brake cylinders. As built, the British Railways-designed locomotives had automatic slack adjusters but the BRCW locomotives did not, adjustment for brake-block wear being provided in the rigging which it was necessary to adjust periodically to compensate for brake-block wear.

Equipment layouts differed to some extent. The bulk and weight of the diesel engine and its centre of gravity determine its position approximately between driving cabs and there is little choice in cooling equipment — again, its size and shape being determined by the amount of heat to be dissipated and by the available space within the confines of the locomotive body. In these two designs, there are also limits brought about by the confines of the somewhat restrictive British Railways loading gauge, the height of which in these locomotives was determined by the requirement of working over the Metropolitan widened lines.

In both cases the same Sulzer 6LDA28 type medium speed four-stroke engine was employed, details of which are given below:

Rated output: 1,160bhp at 750rpm
Bmep at rated output: 150lb/sq in
Designed specific fuel consumption: 0.371lb/bhp/hr
Cycle: Four-stroke
Cylinders: Number — 6
Bore — 280mm (11.02in)
Piston stroke: 360mm (14.17in)
Combustion chamber: Open type
Pistons: Forged aluminium — oil cooled
Mean piston speed: 1,770ft/min at 750rpm
Max cylinder pressure: 1,240lb/sq in
Cylinder liners: Alloy-cast iron
Compression ratio: 12.7:1
Turbocharger: One Sulzer LAG 33-15
Weight of engine: 9.55tons dry

Either type of generator could be mounted on any engine permitting use of spare engines by both classes.

Cooling was by water: two side-mounted radiator panels, one on each side of the locomotive, were provided. These were connected by ducting to a common electric motor-driven roof-mounted fan through which engine cooling water was circulated by an electric motor-driven pump set which also incorporated the fuel supply. The lubricating oil was cooled by passing it through a heat exchanger giving up heat to the engine cooling water.

The background to the development of the Sulzer LDA28 engine range has been given in some detail in the companion book *Class 47 Diesels*, and mention was made in Chapter 1 of one of its earlier versions in the Swiss Federal Railway Class Bm 4/4 locomotives.

In the case of the British Railways and BRCW Type 2 locomotives, the 6LDA28 engine was fully modernised and incorporated such features as oil-cooled pistons, flash-type tri-metal bearings, a viscous torsional vibration damper and a fully-integrated traction governor. As with earlier engines a Sulzer turbo-pressure charger was incorporated and when the British Railways' enquiries for pilot scheme locomotives were issued, the 6 and 12LDA28 engines met the requirements for Types B and C locomotives respectively.

Prior to the modernisation programme, Sulzer engines had been supplied to British locomotive builders for locomotives to overseas orders. For example, the Birmingham Railway Carriage & Wagon Company, in conjunction with Crompton Parkinson and Sulzer, had built 14 locomotives of type A1A-A1A which were delivered to the former Commonwealth Railways of Australia. These had Winterthur-built engines. Six more generally similar locomotives went to the Sierra Leone Development Corporation in 1955/62. However, when BRCW received an order for

12 A1A-A1A locomotives for the Coras Iompair Eireann (CIE) with Metrovick electrical equipment, the engines were built in the UK by Vickers Armstrong at Barrow-in-Furness as sub-contractor to Sulzer Bros (London) Ltd. Except for a few engines, this latter arrangement was to be the pattern for the future.

Now with a large potential demand from within the United Kingdom, arrangements were made for total British production of LDA28 engines with technical backing from Switzerland. Hence when both British Railways and BRCW required 20 engines more or less simultaneously it was decided to build 10 engines in Winterthur and 30 engines in the UK. By those means any early production problems would be seen by both works and could be examined at first hand. That was the theory, but in practice different production approaches meant different solutions, but nevertheless satisfactory arrangements were quickly made by the Vickers engineers who went on to build and test engines at a high rate as will be seen.

The main reasons for selecting the six-cylinder in-line engine for these Type 2 locomotives were low weight, good accessibility and straightforward simplicity with the minimum of cylinders for the output required. It will be recalled that other Type 2

locomotives were produced with 12 cylinders similar output.

The Sulzer 6LDA28 engine is, in common with a of the LDA28 ranges of fabricated steel construction, but to meet British Railways specifications many minor changes are incorporated — such as the use of British standard screw threads throughout. With hindsight, these now constitute a nuisance with the adoption of metrication!

The cylinder block, of the wet-liner type, has a heavy section top plate and is built-up from steel castings, forming the cross members and steel plate. The camshaft is housed in bearings located at the lower end of each cross member and designed so that it can be rolled out complete with driving spur gear in one piece. Three glass fibre inspection panels and two full-length steel covers (one each side of the engine) give access to fuel pumps and crankcase.

The crankcase is also fabricated from cast steel cross members and mild steel plates. There is a cross member at each main bearing position and box-form

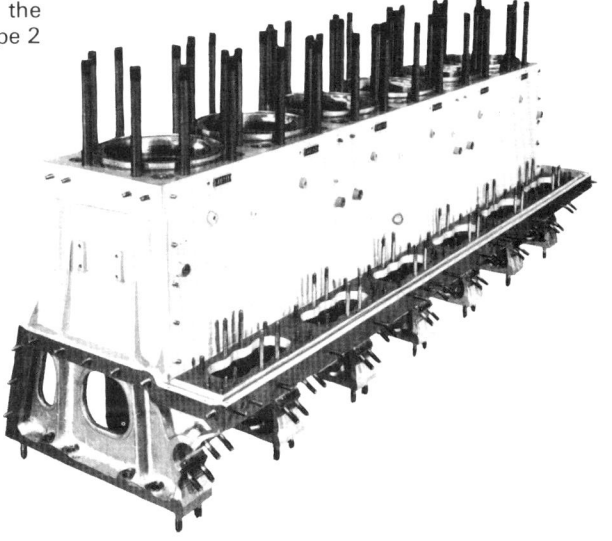

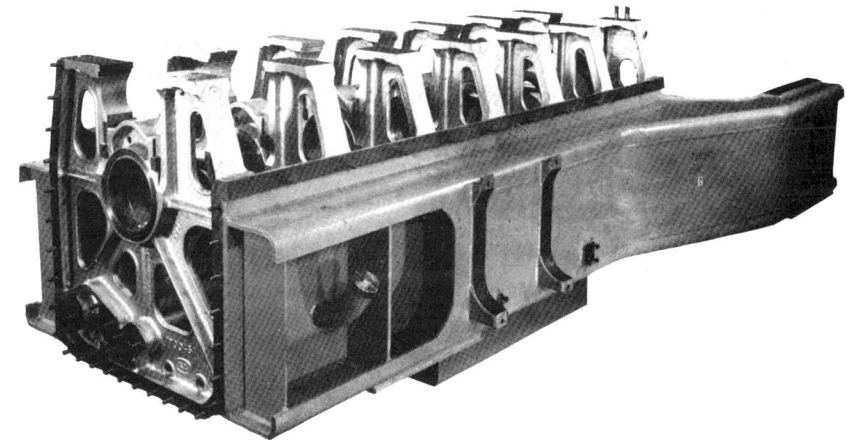

Left: **6LDA28-A engine with BT-H generator — showing separate belt-driven differential exciter.** *Stewart Bale Ltd*

Above right: **Cylinder block, 6LDA28.**

Right: **Crankcase, 6LDA28.**

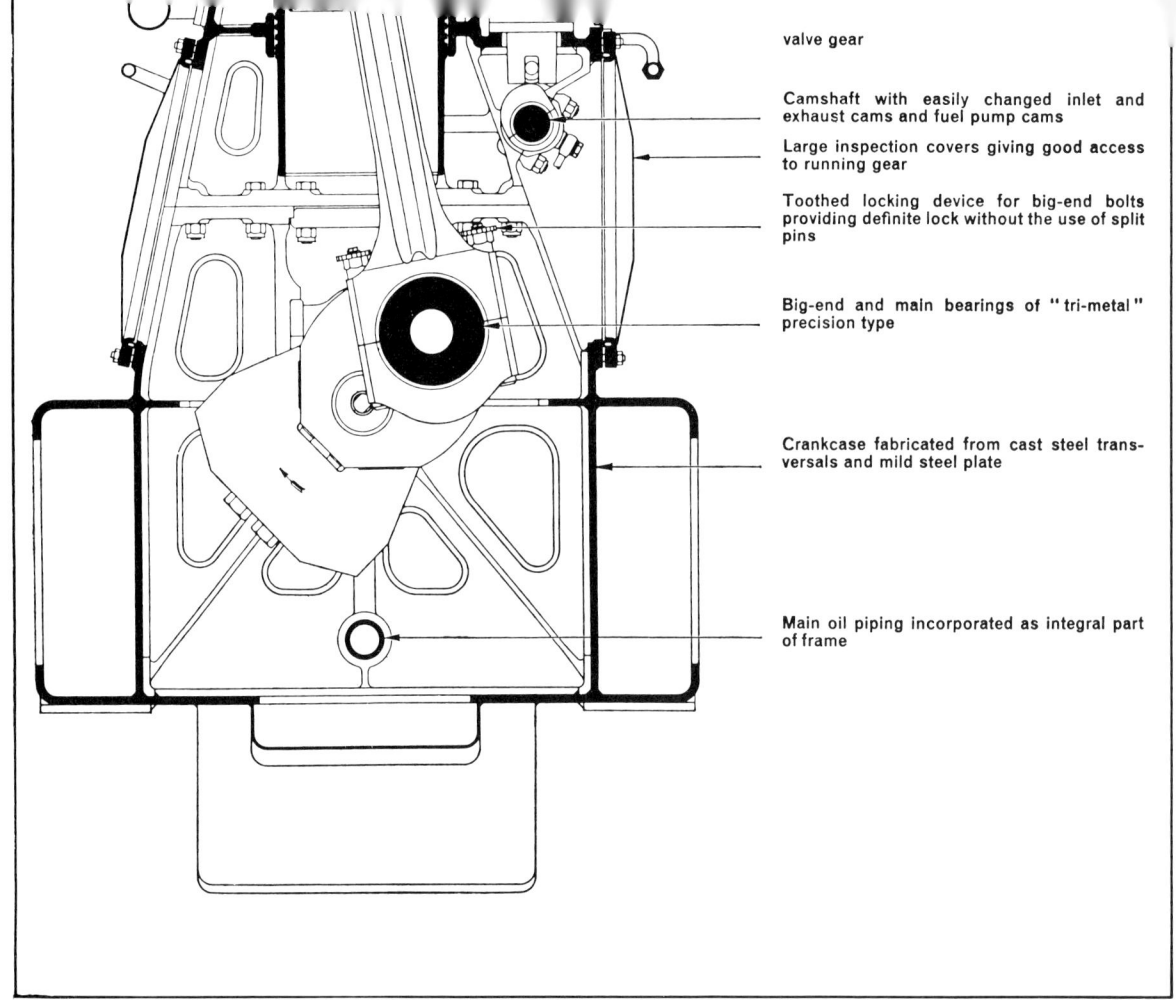

valve gear

Camshaft with easily changed inlet and exhaust cams and fuel pump cams

Large inspection covers giving good access to running gear

Toothed locking device for big-end bolts providing definite lock without the use of split pins

Big-end and main bearings of "tri-metal" precision type

Crankcase fabricated from cast steel transversals and mild steel plate

Main oil piping incorporated as integral part of frame

Fig 4 Cross section of LDA28 engine

22

side girders form the main longitudinal members of the structure, being extended at one end and widened to provide a mounting for the generator. The bottom is closed by the lubricating oil sump and completes the crankcase chamber. The cross members are carried up to cylinder liner level and form the attachment facings for the corresponding members in the cylinder block fabrication.

A cross section through a typical in-line engine is shown in Fig 4.

The crankshaft is of heat-treated alloy steel, fully machined with balance weights bolted and locked in position to the elliptical crank webs. The journals are hollow-bored and finish-ground with the drillings for lubricating oil in the vertical plane.

Main bearings are of the tri-metal type, steel-backed and copper-lead lined with a soft running surface. Earlier bearings employed cast copper-lead but this was changed to sintered copper-lead when higher ratings (and higher bearing pressures) were introduced, thus preserving interchangeability throughout all Sulzer LDA28 engines.

No hand fitting of bearings is necessary and even studded caps are avoided. The lower bearing shell is fully supported by the framing, whilst the top cap is set into the frame and secured by a special wedging arrangement. (Fig 5). The wedges are held in place by toothed locking washers which prevent looseness developing.

A Holset viscous-type vibration damper is fitted to the free end of the crankcase to limit the amplitude of torsional vibrations in such a way as to provide a completely unrestricted choice of engine speeds over the full working range.

The individual cylinder heads are of alloy cast-iron with an open combustion space and porting aero-dynamically designed permitting the use of only one inlet and one exhaust valve per cylinder. The fuel injector is centrally mounted and provision is made for fitting of an indicator to measure the peak pressures obtained in the cylinder.

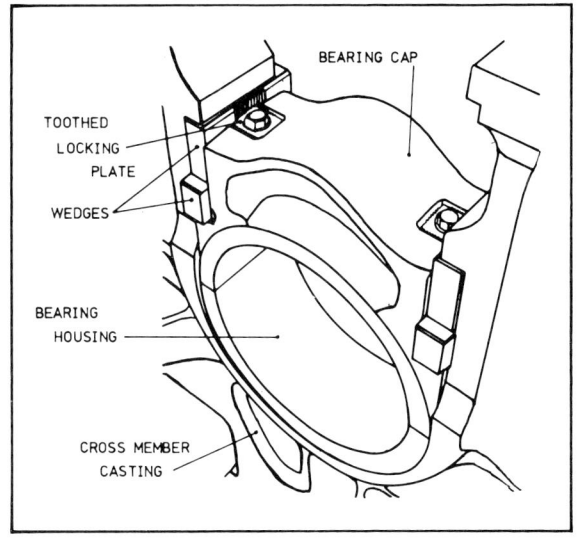

Fig 5   Main bearing wedge arrangement (as for Class 47)

Camshafts, as already mentioned, are built-up from solid single-piece shafts, machined to carry easily-removable cams, which are secured by special circular nuts. Cams can be removed individually from the shaft by slackening back one, or at most two, of the securing nuts. The camshaft, which rotates at half crankshaft speed, is driven by a train of gears from the crankshaft.

Inlet and exhaust valves are operated through a push rod and rocker system and all moving parts, including the valve tappets, are automatically lubricated. Inlet and exhaust valves are identical.

Connecting rods are of H-section nickel-chrome forged steel, machined all over to reduce weight so as to avoid highly-stressed irregularities in the surface of

Crankshaft, 6LDA28.

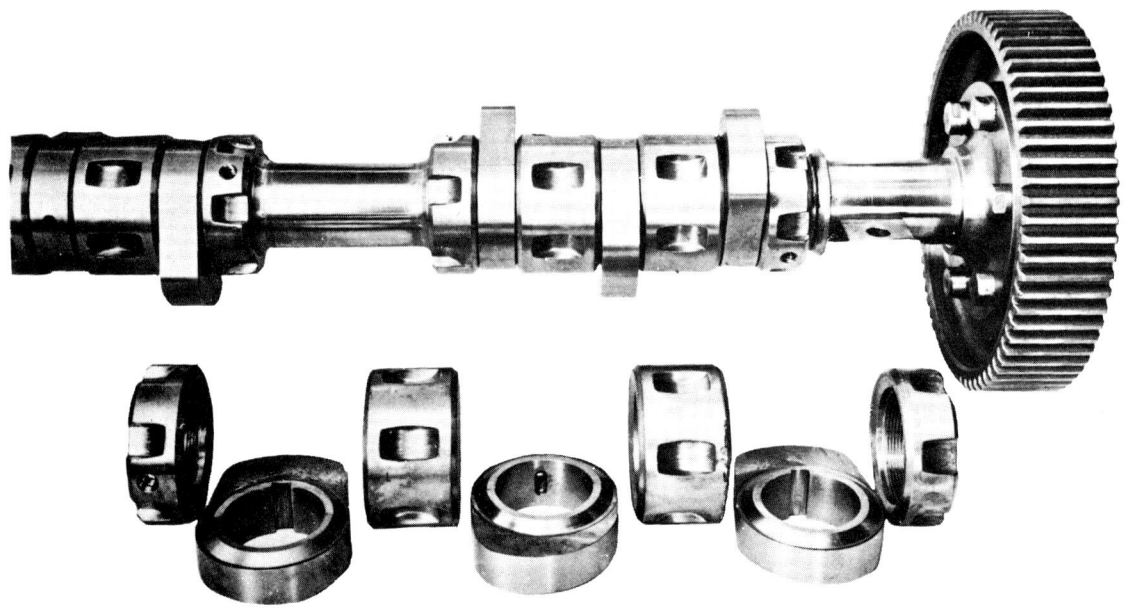

Above: **Cylinder head, 6LDA28.**

Below: **Camshaft, 6LDA28.**

Above right: **Piston/connecting rod assembly.**

the forging and to obtain accurate balance. The rods are drilled longitudinally to carry lubricating oil from the big-ends to the small ends and thence to the piston for cooling. The big end bearings themselves are of similar construction to the main bearings, but in this case the caps have to be located by bolts with nuts locked by a special toothed device, avoiding the use of split pins.

Two piece aluminium alloy pistons are employed, cooled by lubricating oil fed from the gudgeon pin through channels immediately behind the piston ring grooves and afterwards discharged vertically downwards into the crankcase. Cooling of the ring belt is beneficial in maintaining the whole piston ring mechanism free from sticking and excessive wear. There are three compression rings, the top being chromium-plated on the three rubbing faces, with initially copper plating to aid the running-in process. Two scraper rings are also employed, one immediately below the compression rings and one near the lower edge of the piston skirt.

A Sulzer-designed traction governor of the servo-operated continuous speed/torque control type is fitted and driven from the camshaft drive. Its operating medium is engine lubricating oil and therefore is fail-safe should there be a loss of engine oil pressure. All governors are similar with a vane-motor drive to the load regulators.

To prevent the injection of excessive fuel during starting or when accelerating the engine, the governor incorporates an excess fuel limiting device. Known usually as the pressure charger protection unit, the injected fuel is limited to an amount at any time below the theoretical smoke limit permitted in the exhaust. The amount of fuel injected is matched to the amount of air available for combustion, which is especially important while the exhaust gas turbine driving the pressure charger is accelerating to its full speed for any controller position.

An overspeed protection shut-down device is fitted. This is a simple spring-loaded flyweight device which shuts down the engine by bringing the fuel pump actuating linkage to the 'no fuel' position if the per-mitted maximum crankshaft rpm are exceeded.

Fuel is fed to the fuel injection pumps under slight pressure by an electrically-driven transfer pump. It is one of the three pumps forming a unit known as the combined pump set. The other two pumps are the engine cooling water circulating pump and the lubricating oil priming pump. Feeding fuel under press-ure ensures even flow to each of the six pumps under all conditions of acceleration and deceleration of the engine and locomotive. Fuel is filtered first by passing it through a strainer and then a paper cartridge filter to ensure absolute cleanliness.

The fuel injection system incorporates several Sulzer features even through the equipment is manufactured by a British fuel injection specialist. Injection timing control is achieved by utilising a double-helix pump plunger which automatically advances the point of injection with increasing engine speed. The objective is the achievement of optimum injection timing at all engine outputs and speeds with uniform combustion and economical running under varying conditions.

Fuel is delivered at very high pressure by the injec-tion pump through special piping to a connection on the outside of the cylinder head and then passes through a drilled stud. This stud screws into the injector body with a normal high pressure joint. A low pressure joint is also incorporated so that any leakage is taken away by a passage into a special leak-off pipe attached to the cylinder head and thence to waste to prevent any possibility of contamination of the lubricating oil by fuel oil. Lubricating oil is drawn from the sump through a coarse wire mesh strainer by a gear-type engine-driven pump which delivers it to a high capacity strainer and thence to a heat exchanger mounted alongside the engine and carried on brackets attached to the exhaust side longitudinal girder. The engine cooling water is circulated through the heat exchanger and warms the oil on starting and to keep it at optimum temperature thereafter. From the heat exchanger the flow divides, part flowing to a fine filter block, mounted on the opposite longitudinal girder to the heat exchanger and represents only about 8% of the total flow, while the other part goes straight to the engine to feed main bearings, pressure charger, cylinder valve gear, etc. The circuit is shown in Fig 6.

Safety devices are provided which shut the engine down automatically in the event the following con-ditions arise: low lubricating oil pressure; engine over-speeding; cooling water pressure too low. In the event of excessive cooling water temperature, warning is given to the driver by means of an indicator lamp.

These engines are all supercharged by Sulzer exhaust gas turbochargers mounted on brackets carried by the main generators. In the six-cylinder engines, exhaust gases from cylinders one to three are fed into one pipe and from cylinders four to six into another, both being connected to the turbocharger inlet casing. With a firing order of 1, 5, 3, 6, 2, 4, each pipe receives an exhaust pulse alternately. Air from the turbocharger is fed into a receiver which is connected to each cylinder. At full output air is fed to each cylinder at a pressure of 10-12lb/sq in above atmospheric pressure.

While the above basic features apply generally to all of the in-line engines, later developments led to a number of changes. It soon became clear that higher outputs were required on the 12-cylinder twin-bank engines and the in-line engines were brought into line. To distinguish between variants the suffix A was incor-porated and the 1,160hp engines became 6LDA28-A. The next version was up-rated by some 8% to 1,250hp (half of the 12LDA28-B rating) and desig-nated 6LDA28-B. The chief changes were: a new and stronger cylinder head; a higher capacity turbocharger; addition of a small water-cooled charge-air cooler (intercooler); larger diameter fuel pump plungers.

Fig 6 Lubricating oil schematic

Crankshaft speed remained the same at 750rpm. There was a minimal increase in engine weight due to the addition of the intercooler and its associated piping, partly offset by a slightly lighter turbocharger.

As a matter of interest, there is a further variant of the engine used in Australia, Malawi and Nigeria, but never by British Railways. The 6LDA28-C engine is rated at 1,400bhp, 800rpm and uses generally the same details as the 12LDA28-C, ie strengthened pistons and connecting rods; larger intercooler; most other details remaining as the -B version.

Coming now to the eight-cylinder engine, it will be realised that its rating approximates to the -A version, ie

$$\frac{1,160 \times 8}{6} = 1,547 \text{ approx},$$

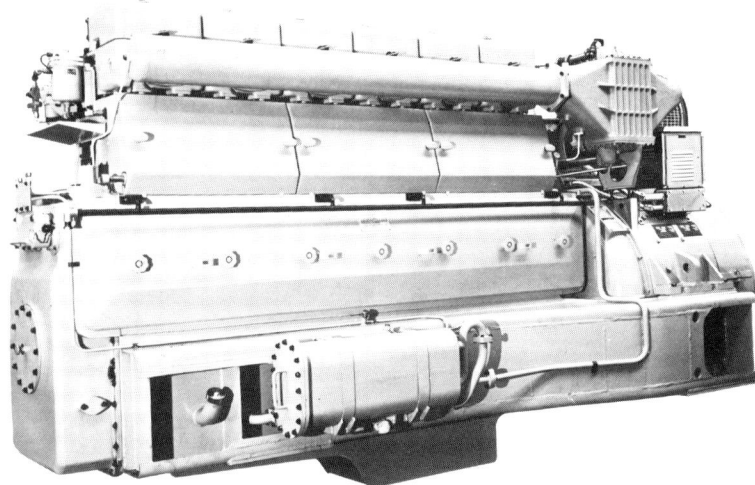

Left: **6LDA28-B engine — fuel pump side.** *Morgan-Wells*

Right: **8LDA28-A engine — exhaust side showing lubricating oil heat exchanger.**

and is therefore properly designated 8LDA28-A.

However, while the main details are identical, some changes were made both initially and later in the light of experience.

Ideally, an eight-cylinder turbocharged engine needs either two turbochargers or a single turbocharger with four entries for exhaust gas. Provided certain limitations are accepted, a twin entry turbocharger can be used satisfactorily. The consequences, however, are: reduced valve overlaps to prevent exhaust/inlet pulse interferences (see Fig 7) with higher exhaust temperatures resulting due to less time for scavenging and slightly more difficulty to achieve optimum combustion over the whole load/speed range.

For reasons of economy, the twin-entry system was chosen and the exhaust pipe system engineered accordingly.

Details of the 8LDA28-A engine are as follows:

Rated output: 1,550bhp at 750rpm
Bmep at rated output: 151lb/sq in
Designed specific fuel consumption: 0.371lb/bhp-hr
Cycle: Four stroke
Cylinders: Number — 8
Bore — 280mm (11.02in)
Piston and stroke: 360mm (14.17in)
Combustion chamber: Open type
Pistons: Forged aluminium, oil-cooled
Mean piston speed: 1,770ft/min at 750rpm
Max cylinder pressure: 1,250lb/sq in
Cylinder liners: Alloy cast iron
Compression ratio: 12.7:1
Turbocharger: One LAG 37-17
Weight of engine: 12.25 tons

Construction is generally similar to the 6LDA28-A engines and all running components are interchangeable.

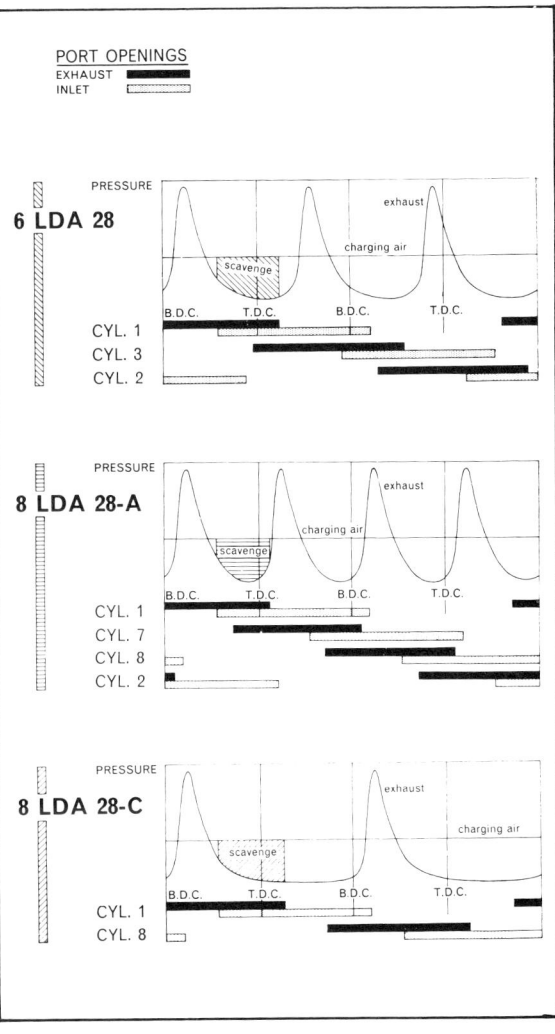

Fig 7   Valve overlap diagram 8LDA28

3 Building Programmes

The pilot-scheme orders were for 40 identical engines of the 6LDA28 type and while building had already been established at the Vickers Works at Barrow-in-Furness, the latest form of the engine developed and offered to British Railways had certain changes incorporated which made it desirable to have parallel production of at least part of the order in the Sulzer Works in Winterthur. As mentioned already it was decided that 10 engines would be produced in Winterthur and 30 in Barrow-in-Furness.

It soon became clear that very many more engines would be required and in anticipation of the demand the Vickers management reorganised the plant and set aside a complete shop for the assembly of Sulzer engines, while component production was very thoroughly examined to see where and how costs could be cut by changes in methods of machining, and indeed by the use of alternative materials in some cases.

The companion book *Class 47 Diesels* gives an account of the preparation and organisation for bulk engine production, but it is worth repeating the salient points here. The first pilot-scheme orders were placed with locomotive builders in November 1955, in this case on Derby Works, for 20 Type 2 locomotives and on the Birmingham Railway Carriage & Wagon Company, Smethwick, (BRCW) for 20 to the same general specification. Prior enquiries and preparation of tenders had brought together various combinations of mechanical parts, electrical equipment and engine manufacturers and Sulzers found themselves in 1956 working with Derby and British Thompson-Houston of Rugby on the one hand and with BRCW and Crompton Parkinson of Chelmsford on the other.

Sulzer engines were, and still are, designed in such a way that they are suitable for production anywhere in the world with general purpose machinery, but the future British Railways programme could be seen to be on a scale that justified the investment of large sums of money on special jigs and tools in order to eliminate hand fitting, wherever practical, both in sub-assembly and final assembly of engines so that reliance on accurate machining of all components was essential.

As has been seen from the general description of the engine, the principal features involved fabrication of the main components, eg cylinder blocks, crankcase, both employing cast steel cross members, and pre-formed and welded platework. Experience with the earlier 6LDA28 engines was invaluable but the future picture indicated the extensive use of pre-machined, pre-bent and formed platework in bulk quantities requiring burning and bending machines on a large scale.

Initial work on the first 30 engines in Barrow followed much the same pattern as the earlier export series, until it became very clear that the original three years moratorium intended to follow the pilot-scheme orders was about to be abandoned. Then a rapid change to flow-line production became necessary and the fabrication department in particular was laid out on a flow-line basis to facilitate production, as was the machine shop, in order to produce the necessary components quickly and accurately to pass to the assembly shop for final erection.

Cylinder blocks were machined three at a time with an accuracy of 0.0005in. The piston design was examined and a change in manufacture introduced so that the production cost and time could be reduced. The piston is made in two parts, the top section, or ring-carrier, is fitted to the body, but was originally welded before final machining. It was found simpler and quicker to retain the ring-carrier by an interference fit, but to ensure maximum security diamond turning of the mating faces was introduced to produce the required finish.

Sub assemblies were employed to facilitate erection, and where possible to pre-set and pre-tested assemblies or components, such as governors, fuel pumps, turbo-pressurechargers were provided to avoid lengthy setting-up times. Final erection took place in three main stages. The first included the fitting and dowelling of all end covers, driving and ancillary components, eg lubricating oil pumps, filters etc.

The second stage was then to completely dismantle the running components and clean the crankcase and cylinder block in a cleansing tank containing a mixture of paraffin and fuel oil, which was pumped under pressure through all internal piping to ensure complete removal of all maching swarf.

The third stage was final assembly, carried out in completely clean conditions. Any engine not being worked on for any reason was protected by strong polyurethane sheeting. Each engine was given full running tests to the requirements of the British Standards Association and British Railways. A testing bay was built to accommodate three six-cylinder and three eight-cylinder engines, or four 12-cylinder

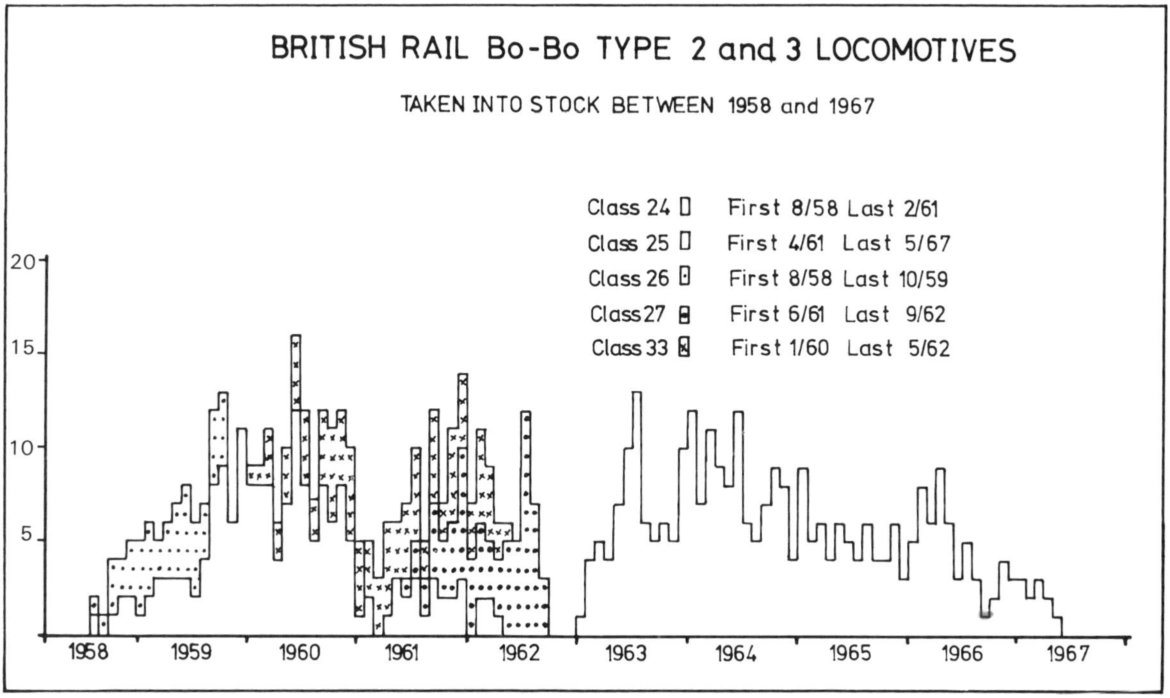

BRITISH RAIL Bo-Bo TYPE 2 and 3 LOCOMOTIVES

TAKEN INTO STOCK BETWEEN 1958 and 1967

Class 24 ▯	First 8/58	Last 2/61
Class 25 ▯	First 4/61	Last 5/67
Class 26 ▨	First 8/58	Last 10/59
Class 27 ▤	First 6/61	Last 9/62
Class 33 ▨	First 1/60	Last 5/62

Fig 8 Histogram of locomotives taken into stock

engines with electrical equipment arranged so that up to six engines could be run simultaneously.

Each engine was first run-in, building up both speed and load to the maximum continuous rating and then tested in the presence of a British Railways Inspector to the following schedule:

Full load	— 4 hours
75% load	— 1 hour
50% load	— $\frac{1}{2}$ hour
25% load	— $\frac{1}{2}$ hour
10% overload	— $\frac{1}{2}$ hour

At the conclusion of the above programme, governor and other components were checked and each engine subsequently opened up for examination of selected bearings and pistons. Only after satisfactory examination was an engine painted then dispatched to the appropriate locomotive builder's works for installation.

To illustrate how the work commenced, slowly at first, accelerated, peaked and then fell right away, the histogram, Fig 8, has been prepared which shows the number of locomotives taken into British Railways stock between 1958 and 1968. It must be remembered that in the same period another 700 loco-

Engine test bed at Barrow-in-Furness works of Vickers showing four six-cylinder engines on test. *Stewart Bale Ltd*

29

motives with 12-cylinder engines were taken into stock and, to complete the picture, it should also be noted that in the same period a further 57 six-cylinder engines were built and exported.

Further, whereas locomotives were being built in four different works and electrical equipment came from three manufacturers, all the engines after the first 10 were built in Barrow-in-Furness.

Below: **Derby Type 2 No D5005 passing Rye with a Hastings-Ashford train.** *Morgan-Wells*

Bottom left: **No D5359 climbs out of Fort William past Torlindy bound for Glasgow, 27 May 1965.** *N. A. Machell*

Bottom right: **No 26.041 passes Hilton Junction bound for Inverness, 7 July 1976.** *C. R. Davis*

Top: **BRCW Type 2, 1,250hp GEC-equipped passes Cricklewood depot.** *Morgan-Wells*

Above: **Nos 33.004 and 33.024 passing Battledown, 8 September 1979.** *A. T. H. Tayler*

4 Development of the Design

The initial orders for six-cylinder engines were met at the then fairly high output of 1,160bhp at 750rpm and, as was mentioned in the first chapter, before the first locomotives had been delivered new orders were placed. For example, the initial order for 20 'Derby' Type 2s had been increased to 114 by July 1958 and the prototype No D5000 ran to Marylebone on the 24th of that month for official inspection by the Chairman, General Sir Brian Robertson. In the same period BRCW received repeat orders for a further 18 locomotives, specifically destined for the Scottish Region.

But perhaps the most significant order in November 1957 was on BRCW for the first batch of 45 Type 3 locomotives of 1,550hp for the Southern Region incorporating eight-cylinder engines using virtually the same mechanical parts as the pilot-scheme 20 Type 2s.

The first of the BRCW Type 2s was completed in September 1958 and was allocated, as expected, to the Eastern Region's Great Northern Line suburban services. Meanwhile orders continued to be placed and BRCW received an order for nine more Type 2s, bringing the total to 47 by the end of 1958, while a further 20 Type 3s were slipped in to bring their total to 65.

In April 1959 a further 37 Type 2s were ordered on Derby, bringing their total to 151. In all there were on order 198 6LDA28A engines. But the pace was now so hot that Derby could not cope with all 151 Type 2s in the time and 54 were transferred to be built at Crewe, with another 20 to Darlington. Two further batches of Type 3 were ordered on BRCW, 12 of a modified narrow-body version for the Tonbridge-Hastings line and a further 21, of the first version, bringing the total to 98 — all for the Southern Region.

By this time it had been possible to assess the performance of the early deliveries and two factors emerged. Firstly that the 75mph restriction could be a nuisance and, secondly, that a little more power might be useful.

Sulzer were already developing the LDA28 range of engines further in response to the demand for more power in the Type 4 range. The same, relatively minor, changes could be introduced on the six-cylinder engines, ie new cylinder heads, turbocharger with more capacity, charge-air coolers and modified fuel injection pumps with an output increase of about 8% to 1,250bhp at 750rpm. And so it went on. Before much experience could be accumulated at one engine

rating so a demand came for more output. Such was the demand from limited resources that what amounted to development work was carried out in the field, because that was where experience could be accumulated quickly.

Although early engine problems were relatively few, it is worthwhile mentioning experience with certain components not covered in the companion book *Class 47 Diesels* because by the time the Class 47 engine had been developed, the items concerned had been redesigned or modified.

Those items which affect engine performance most are usually cylinder components, crankshafts, camshafts or main bearings. Included in cylinder components are, of course, pistons and one of the first problems to arise was discovery of a cracked piston.

Oil cooled pistons were first tried on early LDA28 type engines in the late 1930s and were abandoned following failures in the vicinity of the oil drain holes behind the top scraper ring. In 1955 oil cooled pistons were re-introduced but with both scraper rings below the gudgeon pin. In view of the need for better oil control one scraper ring was again positioned above the gudgeon pin and tests carried out showed positive results, thought to be due to the improved piston shape and materials compared to the earlier 1930s design. Such pistons necessitated the drilling of oil drain holes at 45° intervals and were standardised for the British Railways LDA28 engines.

When well over 100 engines had been completed, a cracked piston was discovered on an engine only six months old and subsequently two more occurred. As in the earlier pistons, failure involved the oil drain holes above the gudgeon pin, which raise the stress in the material at that point, but subsequently investigation showed that only those holes immediately above the axis of the gudgeon pin were involved and that the crack did not run into the other holes, as might have been expected, but turned into the material below them. This discovery allowed the drain hole arrangement to be changed without having to sacrifice the top scraper ring, it being solved merely by eliminating those holes from the area of the gudgeon pin axis and introducing a circumferential collecting gallery behind the piston collar from which oil was drained through six holes in the non-stressed part of the body (Fig 9).

At the same time a secondary weakness was discovered. The piston collar was sealed by a weld between body and collar and cracks were discovered in the weld. These cracks were in no way dangerous, but in the course of investigation it was clearly indicated that the welding had destroyed the press-fit in its vicinity, allowing oil to penetrate between body and collar. It was therefore decided to eliminate the welding and in future to rely entirely on an 'interference' fit between body and collar and a special technique was developed for assembling the two whereby the piston body was frozen by immersion in liquid nitrogen and the piston collar warmed to permit it to slide easily on to the spigot, afterwards allowing the temperatures to equalise when a permanent immovable fit was attained with no possibility of oil penetration from the top.

The modification was introduced on all Type 2 locomotives from June 1959 and many pistons were changed in running sheds and/or locomotive builders' works, eg Derby and Smethwick. The problem was completely eliminated and subsequent piston life has been extremely satisfactory. With the separate piston collar/ring carrier, it is possible to utilise the same piston body throughout the full life-span of an engine and merely to renew the collar when the ring grooves have worn beyond the limits possible for the continued fitting of oversize rings.

One of the important changes resulting from the up-rating to 1,250bhp was the introduction of a new pattern cylinder head. The original head was designed as virtually a square box in plan although it was clamped to the cylinder block by eight studs and nuts disposed in a circle. It was difficult to cast with the required degree of consistency and some sporadic failures were occurring, mainly as a result of this casting problem. But additional strength was required,

not only for the immediate up-rating, but, looking further to the future, for the optimisation which was to follow involving a total increase in output of 20% from the original 1,160bhp. So a new cylinder head was designed in which the forces were transferred to the cylinder block over an area which was in principle circular in plan, utilising the same attachments. In other words it was interchangeable — a factor which was essential because it was to be standardised over the whole range and later replacements could then be of one type only. It was later modified in detail to overcome a cracking problem which occurred much later.

Fundamentally only one other major change was made and that applied really to engines of the heavier rating only, none of which has ever run on British Railways. Owing to the problems encountered on the

Below: **Cracked piston from 6LDA28-A engine (sectioned).** *Morgan-Wells*

Bottom: **Comparison of original A-type (left) and new B-type (right) cylinder heads.**

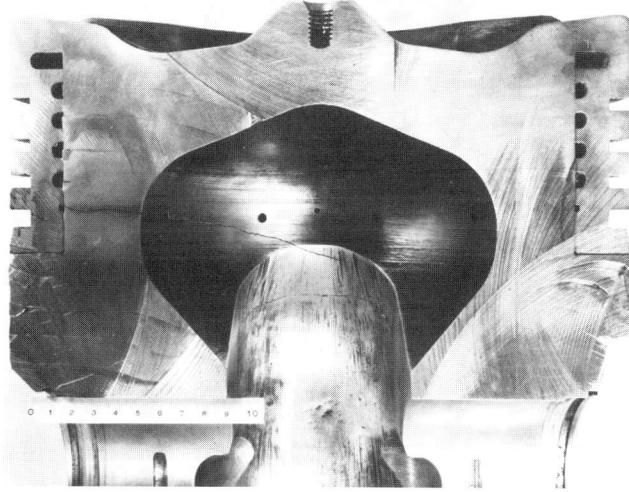

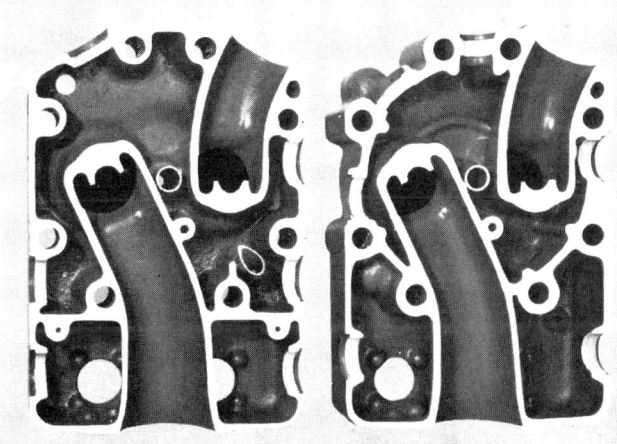

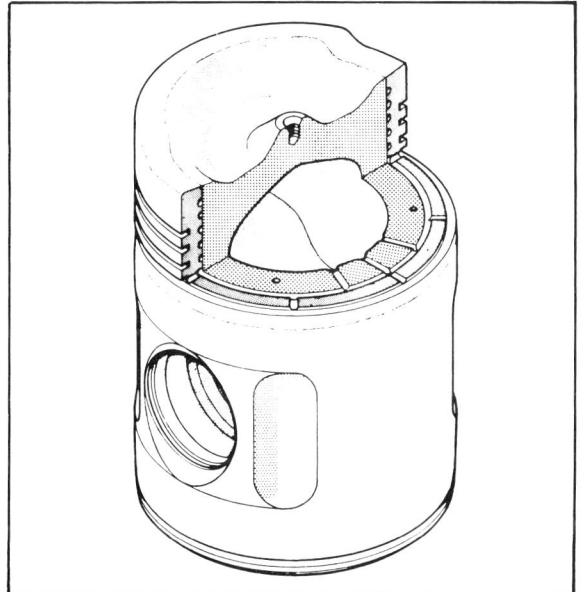

Fig 9 Oil cooled piston

12LDA28-C engines where cracks occurred on the crankcase sill-plates, a new sill-less design was produced and was supplied to Nigeria, Australia and Malawi.

One problem with cracking of a fairly highly-stressed weld did lead to some out-of-course repair work and although a radical modification was devised to relieve the weld of some stress, it was never applied to the BR engines. The weld in question is illustrated in Fig 10 (see also Fig 4) and forms the connection between the plate which carried the fuel pumps and cam follower guides and the intermediate casting. It transmits the firing force down to the bedplate and being a 'fillet' weld cannot easily be checked for uniformity. Also it is in an area where it is difficult to execute properly. While strain-gauge tests indicated a reduction of the weld, stress could be achieved by cutting part of the girder web out, British Railways decided in the end to 'live with' the problem because the incidence of failure was not high enough to warrant attention other than to repair in main works by welding those which cracked.

Special mention should be made of the eight-cylinder engines which power the Class 33 locomotives. It will be recalled that the eight-cylinder engine could be accommodated in the same frame as the Class 26/27 by virtue of the fact that there were no steam train heating boilers. It was decided to contain costs to fit a simple two-pipe exhaust system where theoretically a four-pipe system would have been better. The penalty is slightly inferior 'breathing' resulting in higher exhaust temperatures which bring higher thermal 'stressing', ie the whole engine tends to run hotter. (See Fig 7.)

In the case of the 8LDA28 engines, apart from those problems already mentioned, there were more cylinder head failures and they occurred earlier. A decision was therefore taken to replace all of the earlier design (A type) heads by the new (B type) strengthened pattern which resolved the problem.

Mention should also be made of balancing. It will be recalled that the 12-cylinder engines had to be modified to improve the stress distribution in the structures and more and heavier balance weights had to be added to the crankshafts, while one shaft also had to be rotated to a different angular position to compensate for the effects of the masses rotating. This problem does not, of course, occur on a six or eight cylinder in-line engine, but balance weights still have to be provided to oppose the other revolving masses, the connecting rods and associated bearings etc. Because there was more room, a higher proportion of the rotating masses were balanced in the in-line engines initially and larger balance weights were fitted right from the start.

But because any crankshaft has flexibility and cylinders 'fire' in sequence, the shaft is subjected to twist. Being flexible, the twist is set up in the shaft and then released, which results in an oscillation within the shaft. Such oscillations can cause resonance

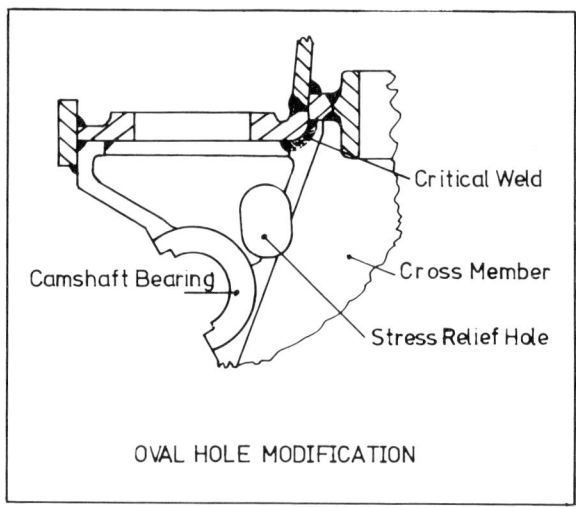

Fig 10 Camshaft tray weld

within the system, which in turn may result in stresses within the material high enough to cause failure. To combat this phenomenon a device known as a torsional damper is fitted to the 'free' end of the shaft — the end remote from the generator, so that at no point in the speed range is resonance producing 'critical' stresses.

Dampers are fitted to both six and eight-cylinder engines which consist of a free mass inside a casing bolted solidly to the crankshaft. The very small space between the mass and the casing is filled completely with a very high viscosity fluid. Because the mass is driven through the fluid and there is in effect friction involved, some heat is produced, but because the driving torque is pulsating to degrees determined by the torsion in the shaft the heat dissipated is proportional to the amount of damping achieved.

Originally it was considered that because the dampers were completely sealed their 'life' would be infinite. Again it should be explained that viscous dampers were, in 1958, a relatively new innovation. But experience has taught diesel engine builders differently. The viscous damper is a proprietary item and its designers were no more experienced in the ultimate effects than the users. Also, some limitations on bulk and weight led to the use of dampers just large enough to be theoretically correct. The eight-cylinder engine is of a heavier duty and after 20 engines had been built, Sulzer decided to fit a larger damper. The largest one which could be accommodated within the engine end casing was 735mm diameter against 725mm originally employed.

In 1966 the engine in locomotive No D6504 broke a crankshaft. Subsequent investigation revealed unmistakable signs of the damper having overheated. It was returned to the manufacturers and opened up and the conclusion was drawn that the free mass had seized on its bearing rendering the damper completely ineffective and the resulting high crankshaft stress had led to failure. A close watch was kept on engines visiting Eastleigh Works for overhaul and it was not too long before other potentially dangerous dampers were found. The reporting of heavy and unusual vibration on two engines in service revealed two more completely ineffective dampers and steps were taken immediately to remove the engines and change the dampers. In both cases also, the crankshafts were examined minutely for cracks, but none was found. However the shafts were suspect as they had been subjected to stresses well in excess of the designed level and would therefore have lost some 'life'.

It was conceded that provision must be made for maintenance and a modification was introduced which allowed for, firstly, the provision of 'sampling plugs' from which a small quantity of damping fluid could be drawn to check for deterioration, and secondly a change to bolted-on covers in place of the previous practice of merely rolling over the edges, so that damper fluid could be replaced as required and other wearing parts changed as necessary.

In the three months following the initial failure a total of 27 dampers were examined: 10 were found to be satisfactory, seven showed signs of internal pressure (bulged covers) and 10 showed signs of overheating.

While this was all in the context of eight-cylinder engines, opportunity was taken by British Railways to check dampers on six- and 12-cylinder engines. Later, similar signs were found on similar dampers fitted to other makes of engine.

The bolted-on cover has now become standard for subsequent manufacture and where dampers have been suspect they have been modified on an ad hoc basis.

The 8LDA28 engines are rated at 1,550bhp at 750rpm and are therefore in the 'A' category with no intercooler between turbo-charger and cylinders. While provision was made in the Sulzer range for both -B and -C versions, none was actually sold. However, all of the British Railways engines were built by Vickers at Barrow, but one engine was sent for a while to Switzerland where some development work was carried out on the Works' testbed during which it was run at -C rating, giving 1,800bhp at 800rpm and at that output it appears in the engine catalogue from 1963 onwards.

It is appropriate at this point to mention another development which, in the event, never reached fruition. In the quest for even more power, and to limit the cost per horsepower, Sulzer designed and began development in 1962 of a prototype for higher outputs, based on the LDA range but including many of the ideas already incorporated in the LVA range. Its application was seen primarily in overseas applications where a straightforward, operator-proof engine, easy to maintain and cheap to run was the basic need. Two prototype engines were built by Vickers and one was sent to Winterthur for development testing, and

6LDA28-R prototype engine, exhaust side. *Sulzer Bros*

the writer worked on it for a time in the first half of 1964.

Rated initially at 1,700bhp at 850rpm for six cylinders and with a development potential to 2,000bhp at 900rpm, it was of approximately the same overall size as the 6LDA28. Two models only were planned with six and eight cylinders in-line. While the cylinder bore remained at 280mm (11.02in) the stroke was reduced to 330mm (12.99in) in order to keep the mean piston speed within normally accepted limits. The designation was LDA28-R.

British Railways were approached with the idea that one of the Derby Type 2s should be fitted with the second prototype engine and development work proceeded slowly in Winterthur until the problems with the 12LDA28-C engines assumed mammoth proportions. Testbed space and development personnel had to be quickly diverted to solving those problems and, as at the same time it became obvious that third world demand for engines was not developing as had been hoped, the 6LDA28-R engine was put on one side. By 1967 it was obvious that resources could not be spared for the development of no fewer than four different varieties of engine in the 1,000-4,000hp range and the LDA28-R engine, having the least potential of them all, was dropped. The two engines were to be scrapped. In the event the Winterthur engine went to Zurich Technical University and the second engine, retained in the United Kingdom, was sold for scrap. Actually it is still in existence and has been used at somewhat lower than its originally intended output as standby power for a department store in the West Midlands.

No D5299 might have been a Type 3 if the development had continued. In the event it was completed as a standard Class 25.

Top: Cross London freight leaving Cricklewood behind Class 24/1 No D5211. *Morgan-Wells*

Above: Nos D7634 and 7671 pass Lamington bound for Glasgow with a relief from Blackpool, 15 August 1970. *D. Cross*

Left: No D6551 (now 33.033) stands in the down platform at Tonbridge in early 1962. *A. T. H. Tayler*

5 The Electrical Equipment

The pilot scheme locomotives, BR-BTH-Sulzer and BRCW-Crompton Parkinson-Sulzer, now Classes 24 and 26 respectively, differed quite markedly in electrical equipment.

BR Type 2 (Class 24)

British Thompson-Houston of Rugby was the sub-contractor for all the electrical equipment of the first 20 of the Derby BR Type 2 locomotives. There had been an association between British Thompson-Houston and General Electric, Schnectady, USA, for many years and the equipment offered by the company had certain features similar to the American concern and some control equipment bore a remarkable similarity.

Fairly conventional in concept the British Thompson-Houston equipment was based on the usual compound-excited DC generator, with a single outboard bearing with the auxiliary DC generator incorporated as part of the main machine, the armature being inboard of the free end bearing and within the main generator commutator. Excitation of the main generator was provided by a separate, belt-driven, differential exciter in which a heavy current winding carries traction current, the 'shape' of the characteristic being provided by modifying the flux through the medium of a separately (battery) excited field under the influence of the engine controlled load regulator. The chief disadvantage of this system lies in having an additional machine, driven from the main shaft, with its attendant drive, brushgear, commutator, etc plus heavy current connections to and from the main power circuit. On the credit side, the load regulator needs only to handle relatively low currents.

Nevertheless, some doubts were expressed as to the desirability of the additional exciter and its drive in

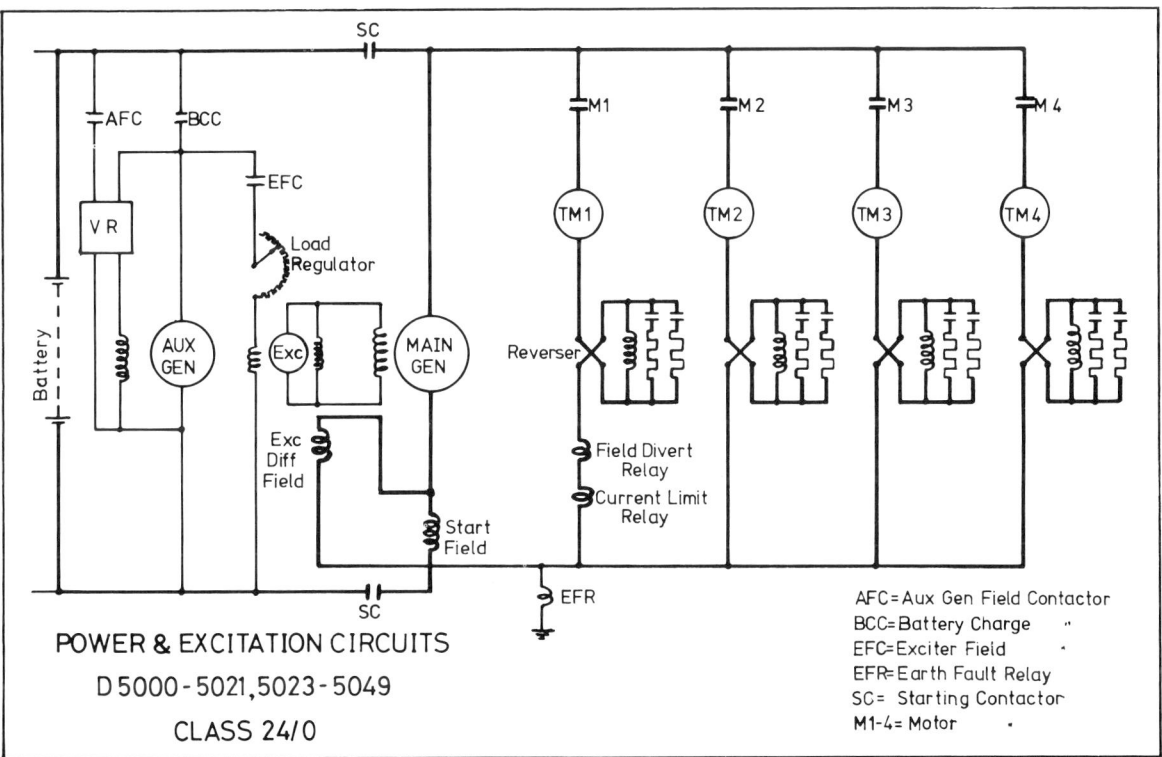

POWER & EXCITATION CIRCUITS

D 5000 - 5021, 5023 - 5049

CLASS 24/0

AFC = Aux Gen Field Contactor
BCC = Battery Charge   "
EFC = Exciter Field   ·
EFR = Earth Fault Relay
SC = Starting Contactor
M1-4 = Motor   ·

Fig 11 Power circuits Nos D5000-5049

view of the fact that other manufacturers omitted the differential exciter from their equipments and No D5022 was modified to eliminate the exciter. Tests showed no disadvantage and from No D5050 onwards the remaining BR Type 2s were built with 'control' field of the main generator fed direct from the auxiliary generator via the load regulator.

The main generator is a type RTB.15656 machine with a continuous rating of 721kW, 1,400A, 515V at 750rpm, supplying direct current to four type 137.BY series wound, nose suspended traction motors connected in permanent parallel driving the 45in diameter wheels through single-reduction gearing with a ratio of 16:81 (5.06:1). The traction motors were conventional four-pole machines with a continuous rating of 213hp, 350A, 525V at 561rpm (14.8mph).

Control gear was the usual combination of electro-pneumatic and electro-magnetic contactors for the power circuits with electro-magnetic contactors and relays performing the control functions. Three stages of traction motor field weakening were provided, controlled by a motor-driven camshaft operated from the engine-driven load-regulator. The whole was mounted in a frame behind the main partition of No 2 driving cab.

Control of engine speed and hence load was provided from a master controller in each driving cab. In common with the English Electric locomotives, control of engine speed was by compressed air, provided by a self-lapping air valve in each controller. This required a through air line between locomotives working in multiple. At zero air pressure the engine operated at idling speed with speed more or less proportional between 7 and 45psi, the latter giving 750rpm. A maximum pressure of 50psi was arranged to provide a small allowance for leakage.

BRCW Type 2 (Class 26)

Crompton Parkinson of Chelmsford were sub-contractors for the electrical equipment. Having no suitable traction control manufacture in their own group, Crompton Parkinson had some years previously made an arrangement whereby traction control equipment would be designed and manufactured, to their requirements by Allen, West & Co of Brighton.

Again, electrical equipment was of more or less conventional execution. Crompton Parkinson designed and built the electrical machines. The main generator of type CG.391A1 is a conventional three-field system, single-bearing machine in which the armature is bolted solidly to the engine crankshaft. Instead of a conventional shaft, the armature is built up on a cast steel 'bottle', the auxiliary generator being on the same 'shaft' with the bearing outboard of the auxiliary generator armature. Rated rather more generously than the corresponding BT-H machine, the type CG.391.A1 generator has a continuous output of 757kw, 1,720A, 440V at 750rpm. In this case excita-

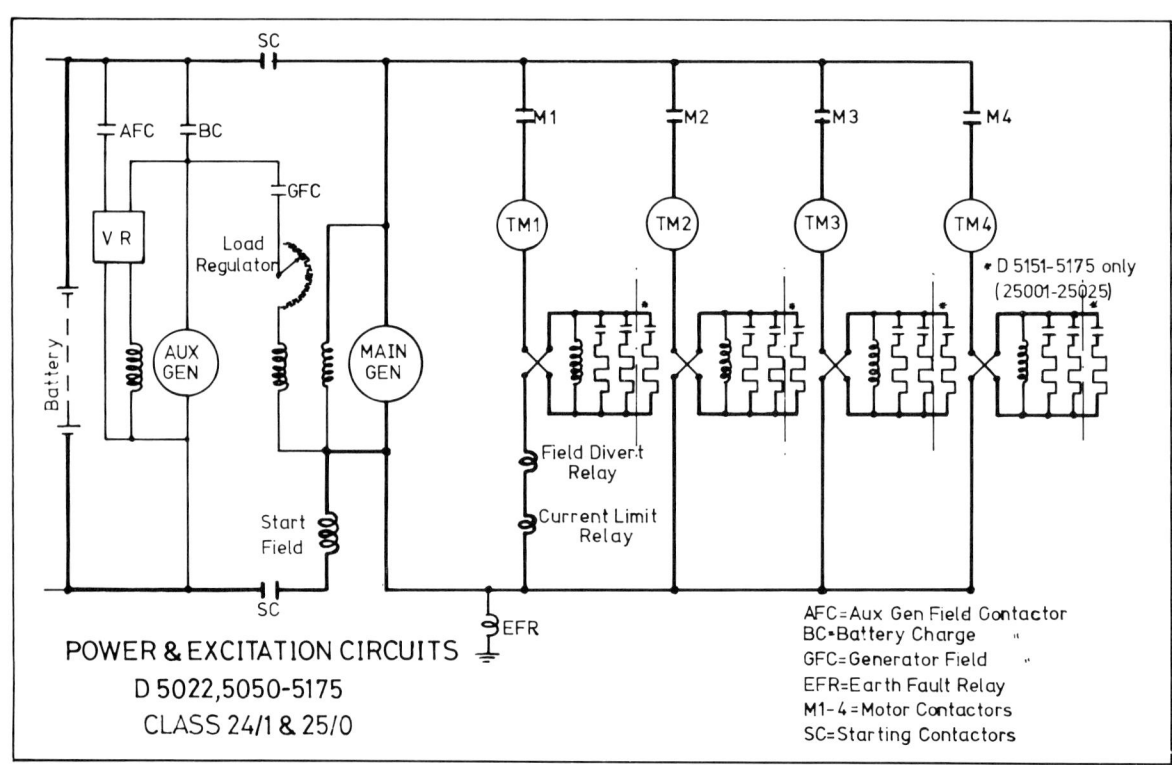

Fig 12 Power circuits Nos D5050-150/151-175

Left: **Control gear for BR Type 2 (Class 24) mounted in Factory assembly frame.**

Above: **Master controller for Class 24 and 25 locomotives.**

tion is provided from the 110V dc battery/auxiliary generator source via the engine-driven load regulator.

From Crompton Parkinson C.171.A1 series wound, nose suspended traction motors, one to each axle, drive through single-reduction resilient gears with a ratio of 16:63 (3.94:1). Connected in parallel across the main generator, five stages of field-weakening are provided from a pilot-motor driven camshaft. Traction motor continuous rating is 224hp, 430A, 440V at 337rpm. Again control gear is of conventional execu-

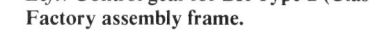

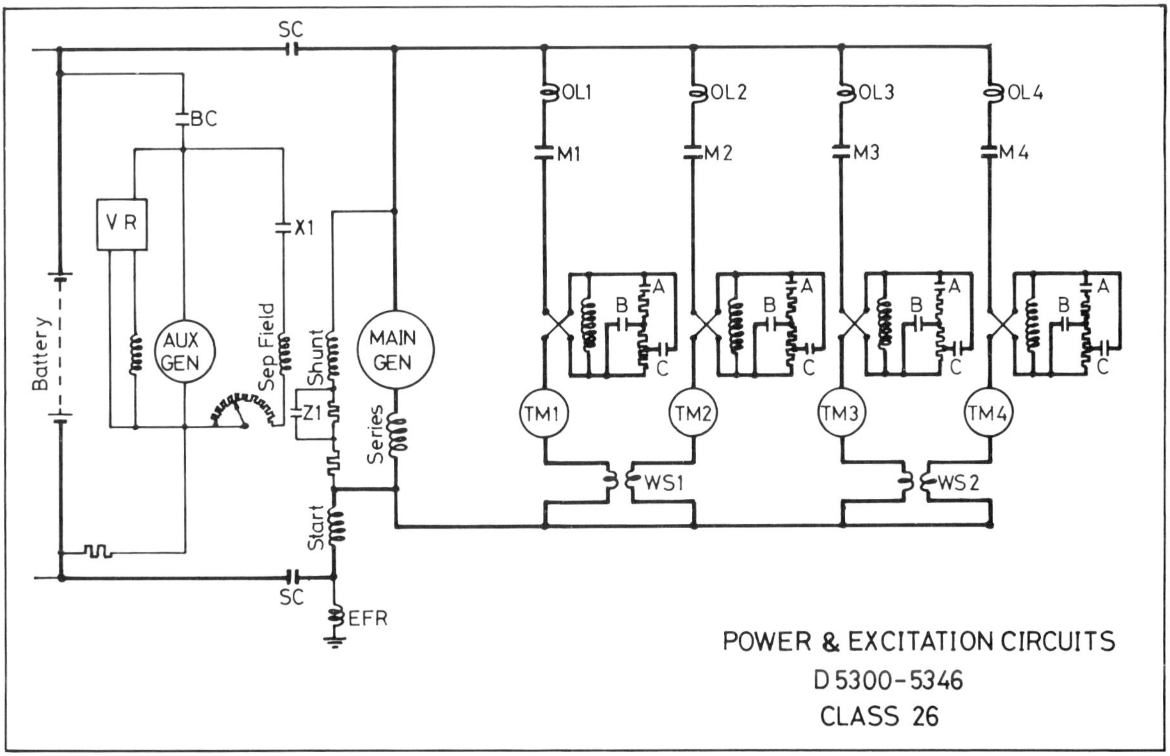

POWER & EXCITATION CIRCUITS
D 5300–5346
CLASS 26

Fig 13   Power circuits Nos D5300-46

tion and housed in a similar position to that on the BR Type 2 locomotives.

Repeat orders for both types of locomotive were received and chiefly due to the fact that early examples of the pilot batches were overweight, grossly-so in the Derby-built examples, a number of changes were incorporated after the first 20 of each. In the Derby Type 2 (Class 24/0) the electrical equipment remained the same, but in the BRCW Type 2 (Class 26/2) a slightly lighter traction motor is incorporated which, together with other mechanical changes, reduced the all-up weight from 77.85ton to 73.3ton. The traction motor is classified as type C.171D3 but the power ratings remained exactly as before, viz continuous rating 224hp, 430A, 440V, but at the slightly increased speed of 11.25mph (347rpm).

The only major electrical equipment change incorporated into the Derby-built Type 2s (Class 24/1) was the abandonment of the differential exciter from the 51st locomotive onwards (No D5051, later 24.051).

Left: **Derby Type 2 (Class 24), view of driver's switch and indicator panel in the engine room.** *Stewart Bale Ltd*

Below: **Driver's cab of BRCW Type 2 showing Crompton/West controller.**

BR Type 2 (Class 25)

When the engine horsepower was increased to 1,250bhp changes were made to the electrical equipment in order to improve the rail tractive effort characteristics which, together with an increase in maximum permitted speed to 90mph, would enable the increased engine power to be fully utilised.

Initially the same main generator and traction motors were employed but with continuous ratings increased. The main generator rating now became 817.5kW, 1,500A, 545V at 750rpm. Traction motors were re-designated 137BX and the gear ratio was altered to give a top speed of 90mph. The chief effect of this was to lower the maximum starting tractive effort to 39,000lb and the rail tractive effort at the continuous rating to 20,800lb at 17.1mph (21,300lb at 14.8mph — Class 24). Full engine output was available from 9.3 to 77.6mph.

This was a compromise solution and enabled an extra 106hp to be made available at the rail at the continuous rating and at the same time extending the operating speed up to the maximum then permitted on British Railways. Locomotives so altered were classified later 25/0 and were Nos D5151-75 (later 25.001-25).

Meanwhile in order to increase the usefulness of later locomotives and to restored the starting capability to that of the earlier Type 2s (Class 24) AEI proposed the use of the smaller, lighter AEI 253 traction motor. This motor had been developed by AEI to cover a wide range of duties on gauges from 3ft 6in upwards.

The genesis of the AEI 253 motor lay in a commercial arrangement between AEI and the American Locomotive Company (ALCO) and under an agreement signed in 1960, AEI became an alternative supplier to American General Electric for the equipment of ALCO diesel-electric locomotives worldwide. For the British-built equipment ALCO specified certain requirements based on contemporary US practice, the emphasis being on more power for less weight. From this Anglo-American association came the AEI 253 motor, an extremely versatile machine with applications from 300hp industrial shunting locomotives to main line locomotives of 3,000hp. But in this application, due to the starting tractive effort required, it was necessary to use pairs of motors in series instead of the earlier all-parallel grouping — a retrograde step since series pairs were more prone to slipping than the all-parallel grouping.

The same main generator frame-size was employed, still designated RTB.15656 with 12 poles. This machine had a maximum no-load voltage of 860 and a continuous rating of 819kW, 1,300A, 630V.

To enable the smaller motor to give the best spread of performance six stages of field weakening were introduced and full power could be used between 7.0 and 77.5mph with a continuously rated tractive effort

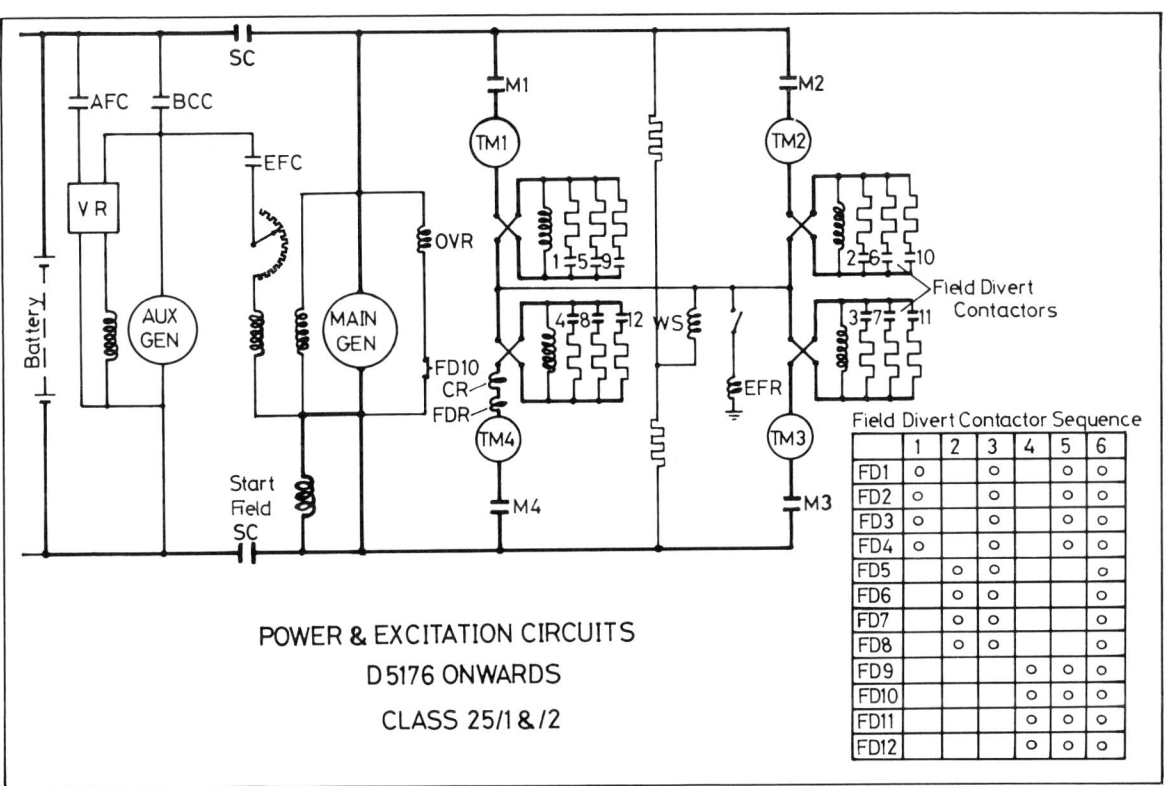

POWER & EXCITATION CIRCUITS

D5176 ONWARDS

CLASS 25/1 & /2

Field Divert Contactor Sequence

	1	2	3	4	5	6
FD1	o		o		o	o
FD2	o		o		o	o
FD3	o		o		o	o
FD4	o		o		o	o
FD5		o	o			o
FD6		o	o			o
FD7		o	o			o
FD8		o	o			o
FD9				o	o	o
FD10				o	o	o
FD11				o	o	o
FD12				o	o	o

Fig 14 Power circuits Nos D5176

41

of 20,800lb at 17.1mph. Gear ratio was 18:67 (3.72:1) and maximum armature rpm at 90mph track speed with 45in wheels was 2,502 while a maximum starting (limiting) tractive effort of 47,000lb could be achieved, although the usually declared figure is 45,000lb. These characteristics apply to locomotives Nos D5176-5299 and D7500-97 (25.026-246 — Classes 25/1 and 25/2).

A further change was made from No D7598 (25.247) when another variant of the RTB 15656 generator was introduced. This is a 10-pole machine with a slightly altered characteristic. The regulated (full horsepower) part of the characteristic is substantially the same as before but the unloading point, that is the point beyond which full power can no longer be utilised, was altered to 900A, 910V (819kW) from the previous figure of 1,050A, 780V (819kW). With field weakening this gives a 'full power' spread from 7.0 to 80mph, while maximum tractive effort is 41,500lb, with continuous rating of 20,800lb at 17.1mph.

With deliveries spread over eight years, it is natural that some changes should be introduced as improvements in techniques are made. The developments in electronics, for example, have led to more accurate speed measurement and indication and instead of field weakening, for example, being operated through contacts and relays, it is now common practice for sequence to be speed initiated. Electronic control of

the the field weakening (divert) contactors is fitted from No D7598 onwards (24.247-327). A signal from a tachogenerator is used and each contactor is closed in sequence at given speeds. In deceleration the contactor sequence is reversed. Thus, at full power, the control system ensures the traction motors and main generator are operated within the continuous rating of the machines except in full field conditions when the driver is able to judge how long to remain in short-time rating condition.

BRCW Type 2 (Class 27)

The same engine up-rating was applied to a further series of BRCW-built locomotives numbered in sequence from the 1,160hp series. Starting at No D5347, building continued onwards to a total of 69, but, due to the commitment of Crompton Parkinson, orders for electrical equipment were switched to GEC at Whitton.

Conventional DC/DC equipment is provided with a GEC type WT.981 generator and four GEC type WT 459 traction motors connected in parallel. Generator continuous rating is 803kW, 1,940A, 414V at 750rpm, maximum regulated output is 811kW, 1,210A, 670V at 750rpm, with a maximum voltage of 715. The frame size is generally similar to the CP and BT-H/AEI machines and in fact any 6LDA28 engine can accept any generator.

Traction motors have a nominal rating of 236hp,

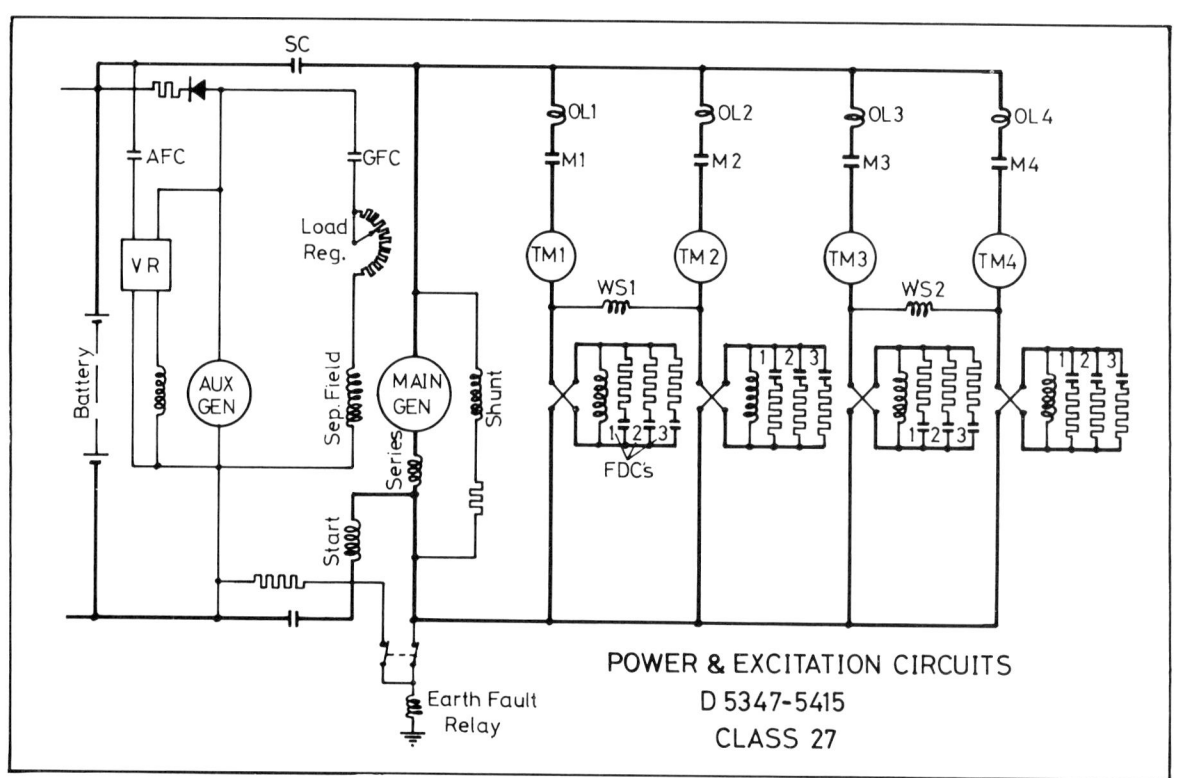

POWER & EXCITATION CIRCUITS
D 5347-5415
CLASS 27

Fig 15 Power circuits Nos D5347-415

485A at 415V, 386rpm (14mph), have three stages of field weakening and a gear ratio of 17/60 (3.529:1) giving a maximum track speed of 90mph (2,484rpm).

Control gear is of conventional electro-pneumatic and electro-magnetic contactors and relays, and housed in the usual frame adjacent to No 2 driving cab.

Full engine horsepower is available between 7.5 and 80mph under the control of the engine governor-operated load regulator.

BRCW Type 3 (Class 33)

As has already been explained, the Southern Region had a special requirement in view of its intention to electrify as much as possible of the system in its territory. Specifications had been issued and tenders from manufacturers received, the locomotive meeting the requirements being the Type 3B as it was originally known from BRCW.

Electrical equipment from Crompton Parkinson and Allen West followed generally the lines of the BRCW Type 2 (Class 26) except that the main generator now incorporated within the same frame three electrically separate machines. From engine coupling they are train heating generator, main traction generator and auxiliary generator. These form a compact group and are all conventional dc machines.

The main traction generator is a CG391-B1 machine of the same frame size as on the Type 2

(Class 26), but with a higher rating of 1,012kW, 1,760A, 575V at 750rpm and of similar construction to the Type 2 machine, the three armatures are on a common shaft of the cast steel 'bottle' form, but of greater length. The series de-compounding winding produces a heavily drooping characteristic which limits the full load current to 2,500A, but a flat characteristic beyond the unloading point at around 1,270A so that the no-load voltage is limited to 840. Excitation is controlled from the engine-driven load regulator via a separately (battery) fed field, which with five stages of field weakening (divert) enables full horsepower to be maintained from 10 to 80mph.

Traction motors are CP type C.171 C2. Similar in general size and concept to the Type 2, the rating is higher at 305hp, 440A, 580V, which with a gear ratio of 62/17 (3.65:1) and a wheel diameter of 43in gives a maximum service speed of 85mph (2,423rpm). Originally the specification called for 80mph but this was increased to the then full Southern Region maximum of 85mph without any alteration to traction motors or gear ratio, at which figure it remains today. Maximum tractive effort is 45,000lb and the continuous rated tractive effort is 26,000lb at 17.5mph.

Train heating by electricity was provided for two main reasons: a) because within Regional boundaries all locomotive-hauled trains would have to be either electrically or dual fitted, the electric locomotives having no steam heating apparatus (other than the

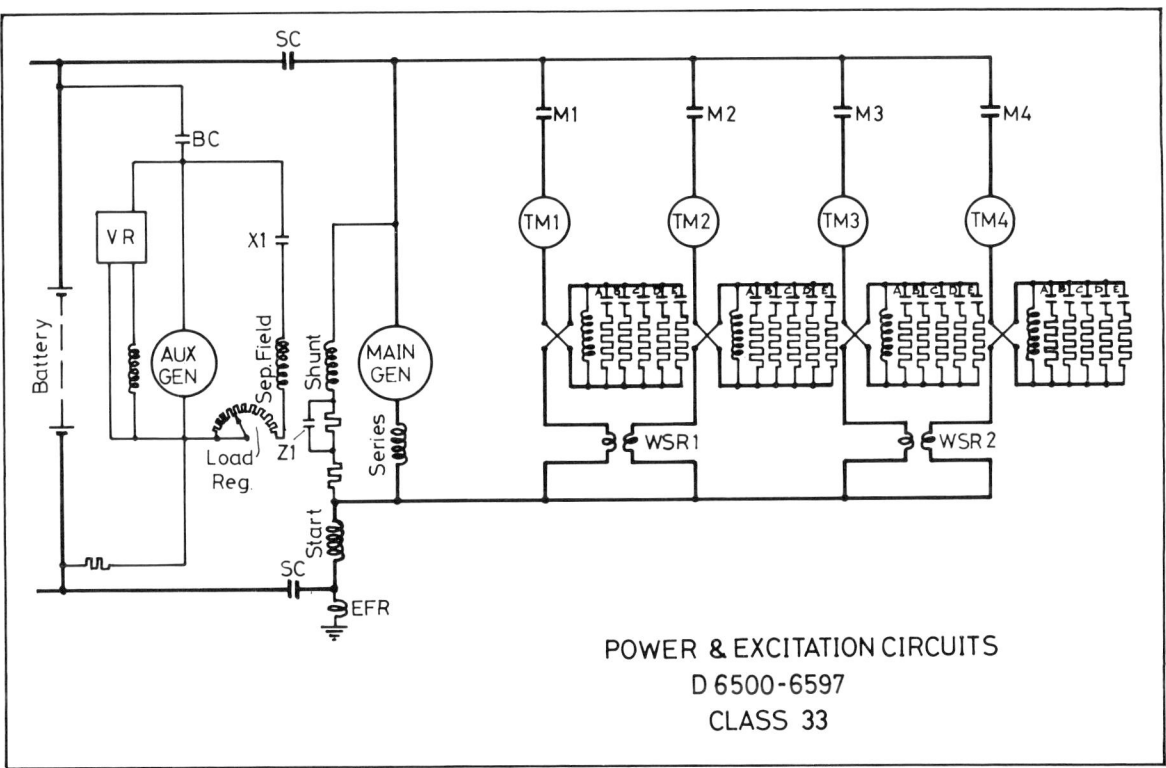

POWER & EXCITATION CIRCUITS
D 6500-6597
CLASS 33

Fig 16 Power circuits Nos D6500-97

three original Co-Co locomotives, Nos 20001-3) and as the bulk of the passenger services would be either electric or diesel-electric multiple-unit worked, locomotives would spend the larger proportion of their time on freight or other non-passenger duties and, having decided to standardise on one type of locomotive, the simplest and cheapest way to heat trains was electrically. That left the question 'how to do it?'.

It was decided to use an engine-driven generator for the purpose. A precedent could be found in the two Swiss Federal Railways Bo-Bo Bm 4/4 locomotives Nos 11451/2 and a similar arrangement was adopted on the BRCW Type 3B (Class 33). Since the operating specification envisaged the operation of passenger trains of up to 375 tons with a single locomotive — 10 coaches — a maximum electrical load of some 170kW would be required at 750V equivalent to about 220 horsepower from the engine. On the other hand pre-heating of longer trains would be required, up to 14 coaches, and even the operation of such trains from time-to-time which could be covered by two Type 3B locomotives in multiple unit so that a larger capacity would be desirable because it would not be possible to use two generators in parallel. A maximum continuous rating of 250kW was finally provided.

The generator is a conventional separately excited machine and is regulated to give a constant output of 250kW, 800V, 313A over a speed range of 550-750rpm. A CP type CG.392A1 machine, it is provided with its own automatic load regulator. This was a small pilot-motor driven device originally and while reasonably satisfactory at or near full ouput, it would hunt at lower outputs. This was of little consequence until the requirement to provide auxiliary power for TC stock arose necessitating a reasonably stable supply. Electronic voltage regulators of English Electric manufacture were then substituted.

It will have been noted that the train heating generator only produces a constant output over the speed range 550-750rpm. Therefore, when heating is in operation, the diesel engine is arranged to idle at 550rpm and this is achieved by energising an electro-pneumatic valve when heating is switched on and the master control handle at 'Off'. Air at about 25psi is then fed through a reducing valve to the governor speed setting piston and raises idling speed to 550rpm. On starting, movement of the master controller handle from 'Off' to 'On' de-energises the EP valve and engine speed falls towards the normal idling speed of 350rpm. At the same time the main motor contactors are closed, the train heating supply is momentarily switched off and restored when the power handle passes a position at about three-eighths of its full travel. This is to ensure a smooth start.

Since at the time (1960) the Southern Region had to handle Continental sleeping cars of the 'Night Ferry' Service — now alas defunct — where the heating system differed from that adopted as standard by British Railways, two different connections between locomotives and trains had to be provided. Also, to ensure that heating generators could not be paralleled, it is arranged that a locomotive jumper plug cannot be inserted into another locomotive socket. It is only possible to insert a locomotive jumper plug into a carriage socket and vice versa.

British Railways decided to adopt a two-pole heating system with a protective interlock circuit so that if a jumper plug was removed from a socket anywhere in a train, the main heating contactor on the locomotive would open and obviate staff handling a 'live' plug. This is achieved by a circuit which runs right round a train and is completed by the rear jumper on the last vehicle being inserted into its 'dummy' receptacle. The UIC system used on the continent for many years is a single-pole system where the negative is provided by earthing all heaters on each vehicle and using the wheels and rails as the return. The control circuits on the Southern Region locomotives, electric and diesel electric, had to cope with both systems and to switch on the UIC system, only the locomotive jumper is plugged into the corresponding coach socket and to close the heating contactor independently of the interlock circuit a separate control button has to be pressed with the 'Heating On' button. This is why the Southern Region locomotives have three buttons on the heating control panel as against two elsewhere. At the present moment of course there are no UIC

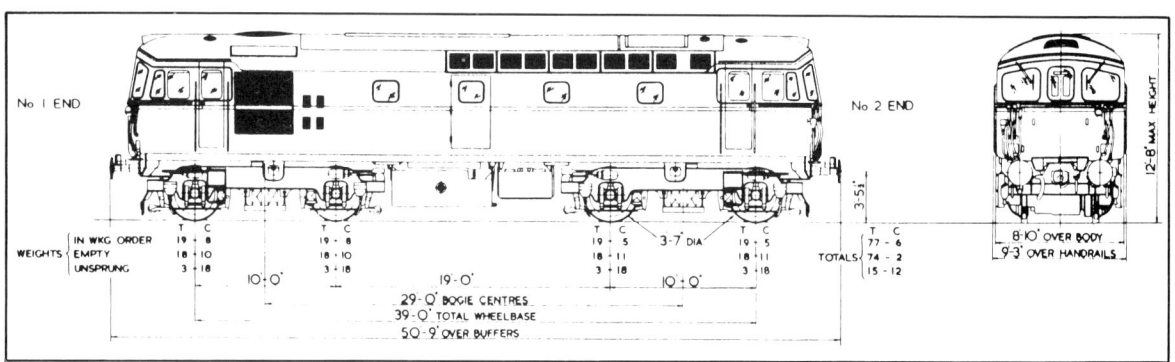

Side and end elevation of Class 33/1.

Crompton Parkinson main, heating and auxiliary generator group on 8LDA28 engine.

passenger vehicles being handled and the two-pole system is used all the time.

Heating apart, the electrical equipment is very similar to the Class 26. As with Nos 26.001-7, the narrow-bodied Class 33/2 locomotives are all fitted with slow-speed control for cement works and power station operation in north-east Kent.

The most important change, or addition, has been the conversion of 19 locomotives for high-speed push-pull operation consequent upon that method of operation being adopted for the Bournemouth electrification. Because the Bournemouth line electrification did not extend to Weymouth, as had been the original intention, attention had to be given to the problem of running 'through' portions of trains between Bournemouth and Weymouth. The solution finally adopted being to use Class 33 locomotives to take forward the through portion, usually four coaches but sometimes eight (one or two 4TC sets). To avoid run-round problems at either end and to cut down attachment and detachment times at Bournemouth, the locomotive hauls its coaches to Weymouth and propels them back to Bournemouth.

In this case, unlike the Edinburgh-Glasgow service, the locomotive control system had to be made compatible with the signals transmitted through the train lines used for EMU working. Also the EMU control train lines were fed at 70V while the locomotive used the British Railways standard 110V for control. Commands from the EMU system also had to be translated into a language usable on the locomotive to control engine speed, and the EMU controller had just four positions: 'shunt', 'series', 'parallel' and 'weak field'.

The problem of the different control voltages was overcome by designing the rolling stock to accept the 110V dc supply from either Class 33 or 73 locomotives, while auxiliary supplies on the TC stock are obtained from the train heating bus lines. Apart from heating, when required, a motor generator and air compressor fed from the HT lines are provided on each 4TC set for lighting, control and brake supplies.

The main alterations to the locomotives consist of provision of waist level control jumpers and air pipes, plus the necessary equipment to translate electrical signals to give pre-determined engine speeds to correspond with the four commands possible from the EMU master controller. One other important point is engine starting and stopping and the former function is achieved through an automatic sequence which, when completed and the engine is running, sends a return indication to the remote driving cab that the engine is ready to take load.

No justification could be made to convert more than 19 locomotives and these are now classified 33/1. In addition to the Bournemouth-Weymouth services, push-pull operation may be observed on Waterloo-Salisbury services and elsewhere under special workings. One other interesting feature is that combined Class 33/1 and EMU formations can be run. One such regular service was from Salisbury-Waterloo which left Salisbury with a Class 33/1 hauling a 4TC to which was coupled at Basingstoke an 8VEP formation from Eastleigh, the whole going forward to Waterloo controlled from the Class 33/1.

Engine speed control, which is normally infinitely variable between 350 and 750rpm, is converted to four fixed steps to roughly correspond with the four EMU power levels. A 'Westcode' 7-step relay valve is fitted which is brought into operation for remote control only, but in this case is modified to give four fixed air pressures of 14, 28, 42 and 49psi roughly corresponding to 430, 570, 720 and 750rpm or 390, 920, 1,440 and 1,550bhp respectively. When operating in this mode, the reduced voltage from the train heating generator is no great embarrassment because the MG set(s) can accept the lower voltage satisfactorily.

Classes 24-7 had similar auxiliary machines, although there was some variation in output between the 1,160 and 1,250hp locomotives, due chiefly to the greater radiator fan capacity on the latter.

Auxiliary generators are provided to supply 110V

dc, regulated for radiator fan motors, traction motor blowers, air compressor, exhausters, battery charging and the combined water, fuel oil and lubricating priming pump set.

Starting batteries are a vital part of any diesel locomotive. There are two fundamentally different types known usually by the difference in their electrolytes. The 'Alkaline' battery with nickel and cadmium elements is not so well known as the 'lead-acid' type which most people know from their experience with motor cars. Both have their special characteristics, the chief being that 'Alkaline' batteries have a high first cost but a long life expectancy, while 'lead-acid' batteries have a known relatively short life but at a correspondingly lower first cost. They also perform better at low ambient temperatures and there are other advantages and disadvantages.

Initially orders for both classes of Type 2 were built with 'alkaline' batteries and these were perpetuated throughout the Class 26 and 27s. The Derby-built Type 2 retained 'alkaline' batteries for a time but pressure from within the British Railways organisation to use batteries manufactured at their own Wolverton Works led to later batches having batteries of that type. It appears that under British Railways conditions there is no clear-cut advantage either way.

The Type 3 (Class 33) locomotives employed lead-acid batteries from the start, although a reduction in size and weight was made at an early stage and doubts about capacity were dispelled by carrying out a series of repeated starting tests at low ambient temperature which proved the design.

One main point of difference between the Crompton equipped locomotives and the others is the use of electro-pneumatic starting contactors on Classes 26 and 33 which require an air pressure of at least 40psi to be raised before an engine start can be made. This involved running the main air compressor from the battery before starting, in addition to the combined water, fuel, lubricating pump set. If the battery is in a run-down state, or nearing the end of its life, or indeed if repeated starts have to be made in a short period, failure to start, or failure to close the contactors can occur. Due to the heavier starting duty with the eight-cylinder engines or the Class 33s, electro-magnetic contactors were later substituted and the air compressor does not now have to be run.

Below: **Class 33/1 locomotive No 33.112 propelling a 4TC unit past Battledown Junction in October 1980.** *A. T. H. Tayler*

Bottom: **Glasgow-Inverness train near Slochd behind two BRCW Type 2s.** *Morgan-Wells*

6 Performance and Utilisation

The original 'B' type locomotive specifications were intended to lead manufacturers to offer locomotives which were the equivalent of ex-LMS Class 4 2-6-4Ts and similar locomotives produced by the other pre-Nationalised companies together with locomotives of similar capacity in the British Railways standard range. Use of these locomotives on suburban and semi-fast trains was a foregone conclusion, while the power would be sufficient to work freight trains in the faster, medium weight category.

Tractive effort/speed characteristics of both the British Railways/British Thompson-Houston and BRCW builds are included as Figs 17 and 18. While the BRCW-built locomotives were put to work on outer-suburban services on the Great Northern line out of King's Cross, the Derby-built locomotives were sent

to the Southern Region and were employed initially in the Ashford-Dover-Ramsgate area on freight and local passenger workings. One is shown here and is seen approaching Minster Junction with an Ashford-Ramsgate via Canterbury East stopping train.

Between May and June 1959, No D5008 was used for dynamometer car tests, the results of which were published as one of a series of British Railways Test Bulletins which, for the price of 10 shillings (50p) were available to the general public. Bulletin No 21 described in detail the tests carried out to establish performance, efficiency, fuel consumption, etc. Fig 19 is taken from the report and shows the power distribution from engine to drawbar, as measured during the tests.

No comparable tests were carried out with the BRCW-built locomotives because, as the report states: 'In the case of the remaining 47 locomotives built by the Birmingham Railway Carriage & Wagon Co Ltd, Crompton Parkinson electrical equipment has been

No D5002 on Ashford-Ramsgate train approaching Minster Junction, January 1960. *A. T. H. Tayler*

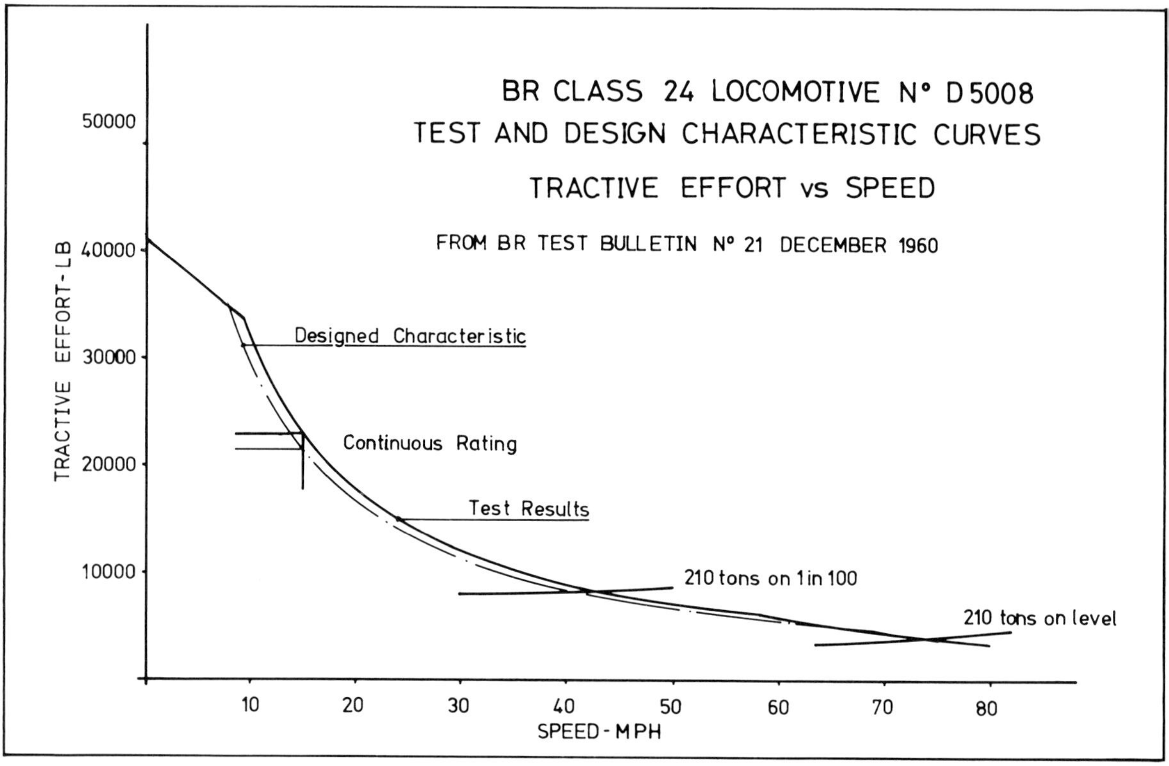

Fig 17 No D5008 performance from tests

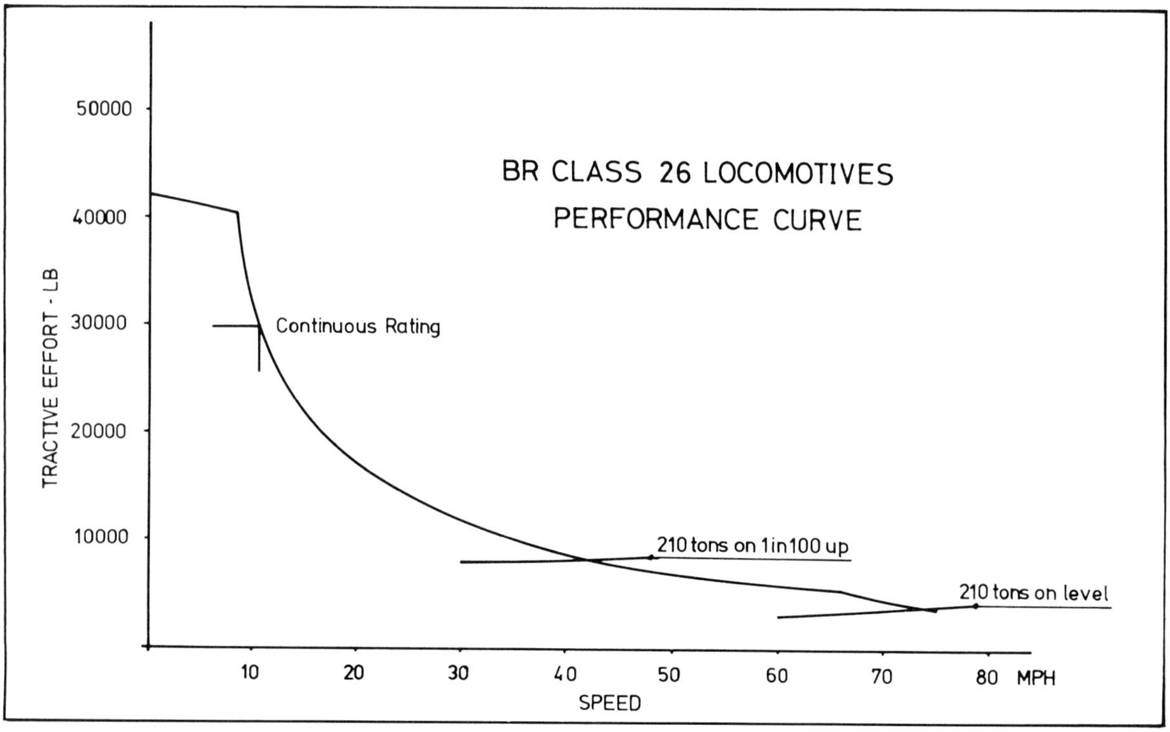

Fig 18 Class 26 performance curves

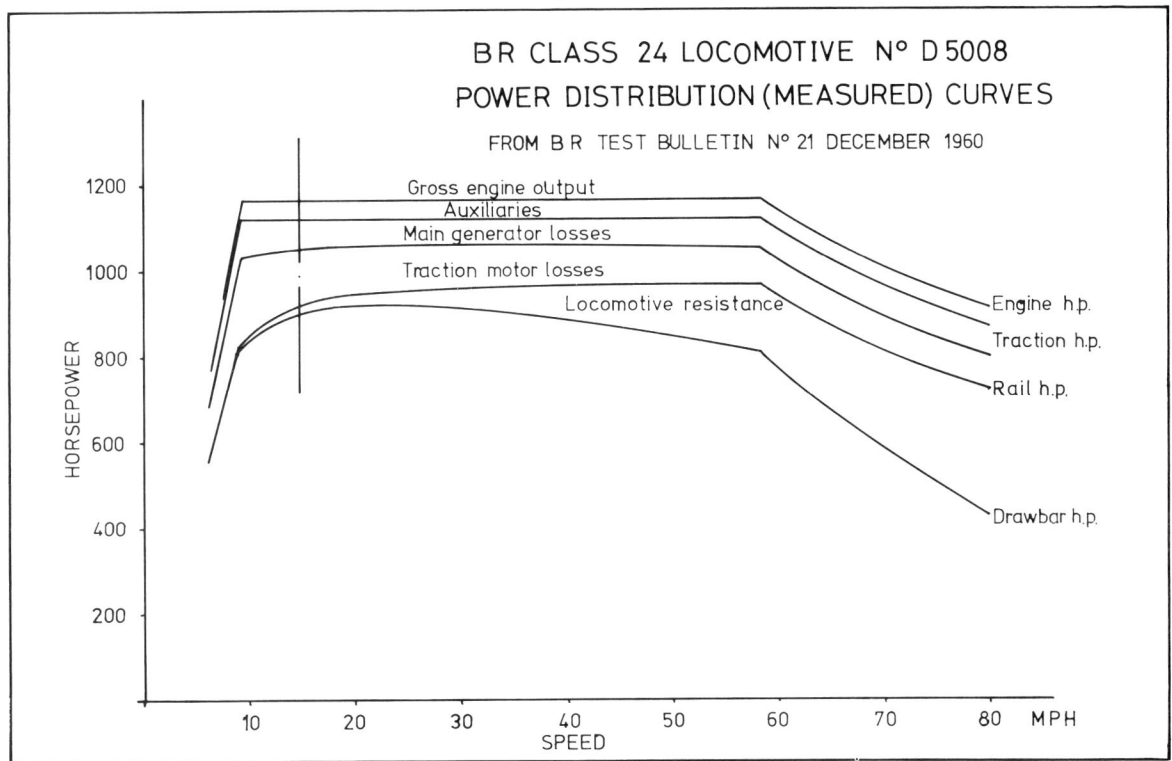

Fig 19 Power distribution Class 24

used. There is no separate exciter and the main generator is provided with separately excited, self-excited and decompounding windings; the resulting generator characteristics differ somewhat from those for the railway-built locomotives with AEI electrical equipment, which gives the designed generator characteristic at full engine power for the BRC&W locomotive. The traction motor characteristics also differ from those for the railway-built locomotives, and the rail tractive effort-speed characteristics are different, particularly at the low speed end. Thus none of the results given in this bulletin, except those relating purely to the diesel engine, are applicable to the BRC&W locomotives. It is, however, again reasonable to assume that the resistance of the locomotive will be the same as for the one which has been tested; hence the same data can be used in conjunction with the designed rail tractive effort curve to arrive at an estimate of the drawbar tractive effort.'

In practice, the BRCW/Crompton locomotives, Class 26, have had the reputation of being better performers than the Class 24s. Why this should be the case is not clear since, while the tractive effort characteristics of the Class 26 are marginally better than the Class 24, the same engine and governor are employed in each case.

The work of the smaller mixed traffic locomotives is never particularly spectacular and it is not surprising that there is relatively little published data available

covering their earlier exploits. However, the examples included here give some idea of the capabilities of the Class 24s.

Most of the Class 26s survive and are still employed in the Scottish Region. From their early duties, which include the King's Cross-Cambridge Buffet Car trains, through their earlier Scottish Region workings, which often involved working in pairs in multiple, to their present-day duties, the logs included here illustrate their capabilities — often indistinguishable from their more-powerful Class 27 sisters.

While the Class 24s (Derby Type 2) ultimately numbered 151, the 48th product from BRCW received different power equipment. In addition to the uprated engine, the electrical equipment was of GEC (Whitton) manufacture. The Class 25s, which continued with British Thompson-Houston/AEI electrical equipment, also received the uprated engine and while, incidentally, having the same traction motors these were later changed, as mentioned already, to the more modern 'universal' AEI 253. The characteristics were slightly changed and Figs 20 and 21 show the designed characteristics of both forms of Class 25 and Class 27 respectively. One other important change in the Class 25s and 27s was the increase in the maximum permitted speed from 75mph (80mph Class 26) to 90mph. The 75mph figure had led to some inhibition on passenger workings, particularly

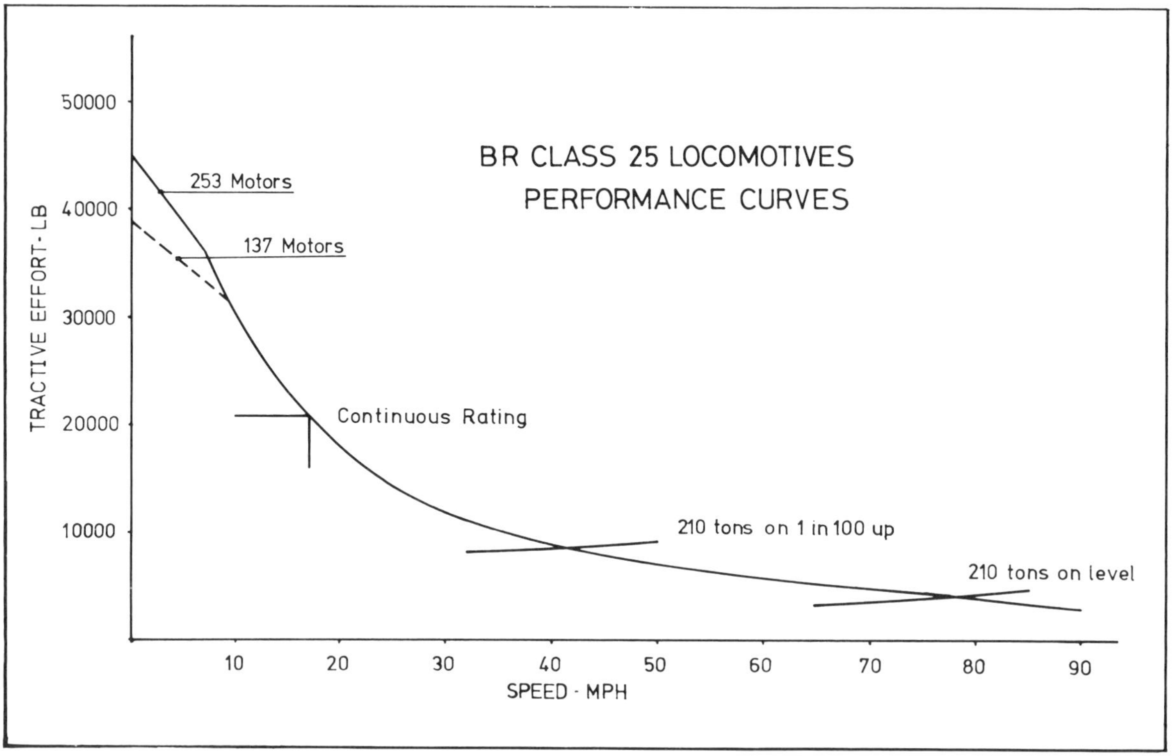

Fig 20 Class 25 performance

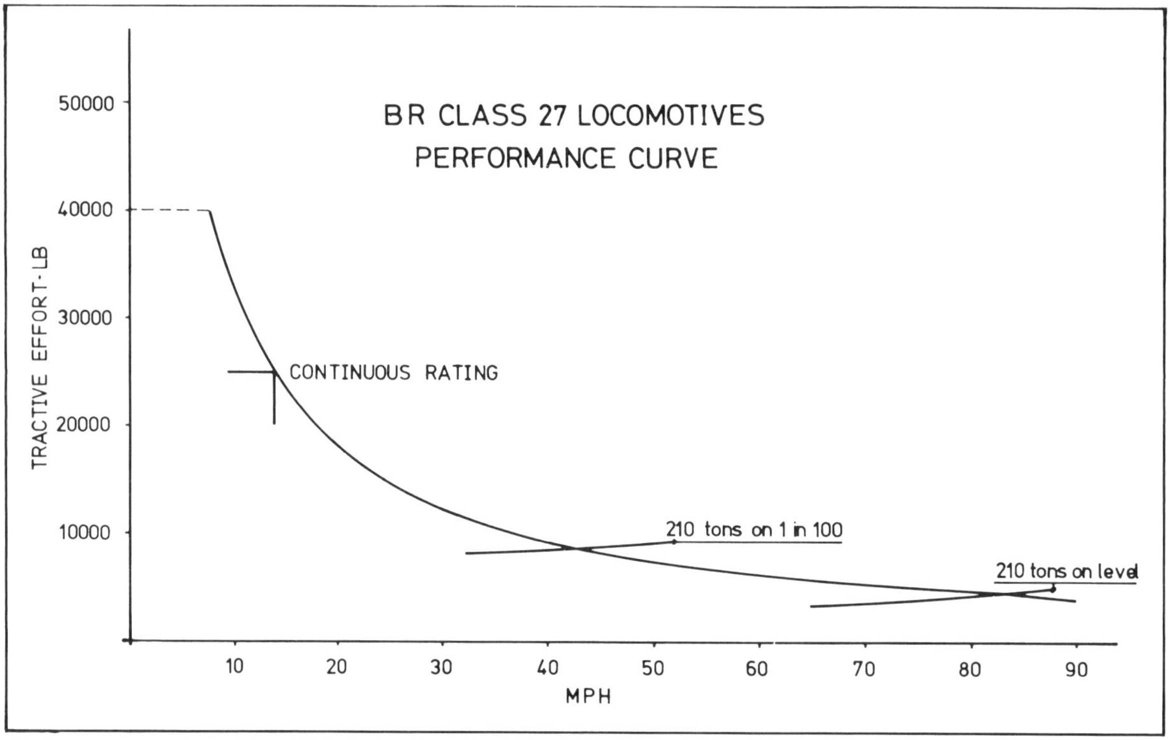

Fig 21 Class 27 performance

when working in pairs as substitutes for Type 4 power or on special workings on main lines where a line speed of 90mph was permitted, and resulted in greater headways being required.

In total 151 locomotives of 1,160hp and 327 of 1,250hp were produced to BR designs. Forty-seven locomotives of 1,160hp and 69 of 1,250hp completed the BRCW production. Since, at time of peak production, many of these locomotives were substituted for steam on existing duties and in spite of the better utilisation possible, it was often found impossible to achieve better than 100 miles or so in a week on pure pick-up or 'trip' workings.

Although allocated originally to three Regions, the Class 24 eventually gravitated to the London Midland and Scottish Regions where they could be found usually on the lighter passenger and parcel trains and on mainly local freight. With the demise of the latter, much of their work disappeared and they were, in consequence, the first complete class to be eliminated. Perhaps their inferior performance and reliability helped while a number of features, mainly affecting maintenance, aided their early demise compared to the Class 26, still very popular in the Scottish Region.

The Class 25s inherited a number of features, particularly in mechanical design, from the Class 24, and of course their shortcomings also. The main frame design for example is weak ahead of the bogie centres compared with the BRCW design, and while their reliability has never been as great, the enhanced power available from the 1,250bhp engine did give them a greater range of operation. Again, changing patterns of operation have rendered many redundant, and multiple-unit working has never in the UK been either very economic or popular, although it is often resorted to with heavy trains, notably in the London Midland and Scottish Regions where pairs of Class 25 or combinations of 25s and 27s are still not uncommon.

While, in their heyday, Class 25s could be seen on four out of the five regions, they too are now confined to the London Midland and Scottish. Never very popular in the Western Region, they were sent to South Wales and Cornwall as substitutes for the smaller diesel-hydraulics, and while satisfactory on china clay duties in Cornwall, were never very happy on the iron ore or coal workings in South Wales, their traction motor capacity being a limiting factor, and especially those with series/parallel connected machines. Some motor overheating occurred due to a combination of the very limited short-time rating of the AEI 253 motors, variations in field-divert relay settings and limited adhesion, not aided by the poorer adhesion characteristics of motors in series.

In Scotland, the Class 25s never seem to show equivalent performance to the Class 27s, and at times even Class 26s.

It is in Scotland that Class 26 and 27s can currently be seen on a higher proportion of passenger workings than elsewhere and, in proportion to their numbers,

both classes are still well represented, having suffered relatively few withdrawals.

It was probably never envisaged that one of their duties would be a short high-speed working which fell to certain members of Class 27 when they were hastily modified to work one at each end of a rake of six Mk II coaches on the Edinburgh-Glasgow route. These workings quickly showed up some traction motor weaknesses and a number of failures of banding wire occurred leading to modification, together with brush gear supports and, to eliminate some vibration, the motor suspensions also. Other problems occurred with bogies and brake gear and even gearwheels which were replaced by others of a strengthened pattern. Since cases of speeds in excess of the permitted maximum were known, it is not surprising that locomotives designed originally for schedules requiring speeds in the 70-80mph range needed strengthening for sustained speeds of 90mph and more. Class 27s were supplanted on the Edinburgh-Glasgow workings at the end of 1979 when push-pull fitted Class 47/7s became available, together with Mk III coaches and modified Mk II driving trailers.

As mentioned already, the Class 33 performance parameters were clearly laid down at the enquiry stage. With electrification in Kent, Sussex and later Hampshire, they have a wide range of duties. At the ordering stage it was not envisaged that they would have virtually express passenger duties, but as soon as the first were delivered they were put to work as substitutes for steam on Charing Cross-Cannon Street-Dover-Ramsgate trains via Tonbridge. In winter they worked in multiple with a Class 24 to provide steam heating, because electrically heated coaches were not then available. They also took over very quickly from steam as many freight workings as possible to enable some steam depots to be closed, eg Ramsgate, Dover and Ashford.

By 1962 they were working as far afield as York on the Holborough (Cliffe, Kent) to Uddingstone bulk cement trains, in pairs initially, hauling 28 bulk cement wagons. By April of 1962, transfer to Eastleigh of nine locomotives had taken place for working the Fawley-Bromford Bridge oil trains in place of BR Class 9 2-10-0 locomotives. They also began to appear as substitutes for ageing steam locomotives on boat trains and other special duties.

In February 1961 No D6504 was borrowed to work a special train between Ferme Park and Edinburgh composed of seven electrically heated vehicles of various types for an initial running trial prior to full scale dual fitting of Mk I coaches for the London Midland West Coast main line electrification. The train ran each night for four nights to a fast schedule.

Again one was borrowed for freightliner vehicle tests which took place between Derby and Leicester. No D6553 went to Derby for static brake tests on 9 January 1964 and hauled the special test train with a dynamometer car for several days, commencing on

D6504

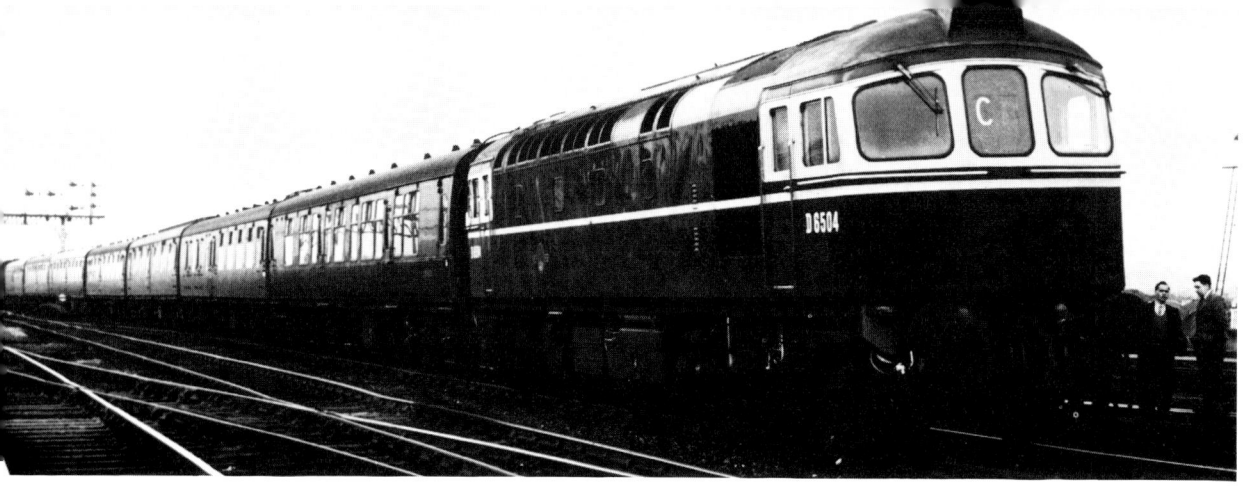

No D6504 on arrival at Hornsey from Derby with seven trial electrically heated BR Mark 1 coaches. *A. T. H. Tayler*

16 January 1964. A Class 33 was essential motive power as no other class was at that time fitted to work air-braked trains!

Having 33% more power for the same weight as the Type 2s resulted in a very versatile locomotive. For interest Fig 22 shows the performance characteristics, while Fig 23 shows the same curves with rarely-published (and difficult to find) curves for a 'Schools' class working at a constant 25% cut off with full regulator and a 'U' class 2-6-0, perhaps the true steam equivalent. Compared to the 2-6-0 at its boiler limit, the Class 33 shows a marked advantage in capability.

While ubiquitous on the Southern Region, the Class 33 have spread their wings to other areas. On 4 October 1971 the Waterloo-Exeter trains were handed over to Class 33 working and did well on these duties with 7-9 coach formations until the need arose to accelerate these trains when in June 1980, Class 50s took over the Exeter workings, reverting to Western Region power and the Class 33s handled the intermediate Waterloo-Salisbury trains.

Other inter-regional workings take Class 33s as far from home as Cardiff and now Crewe. In the latter

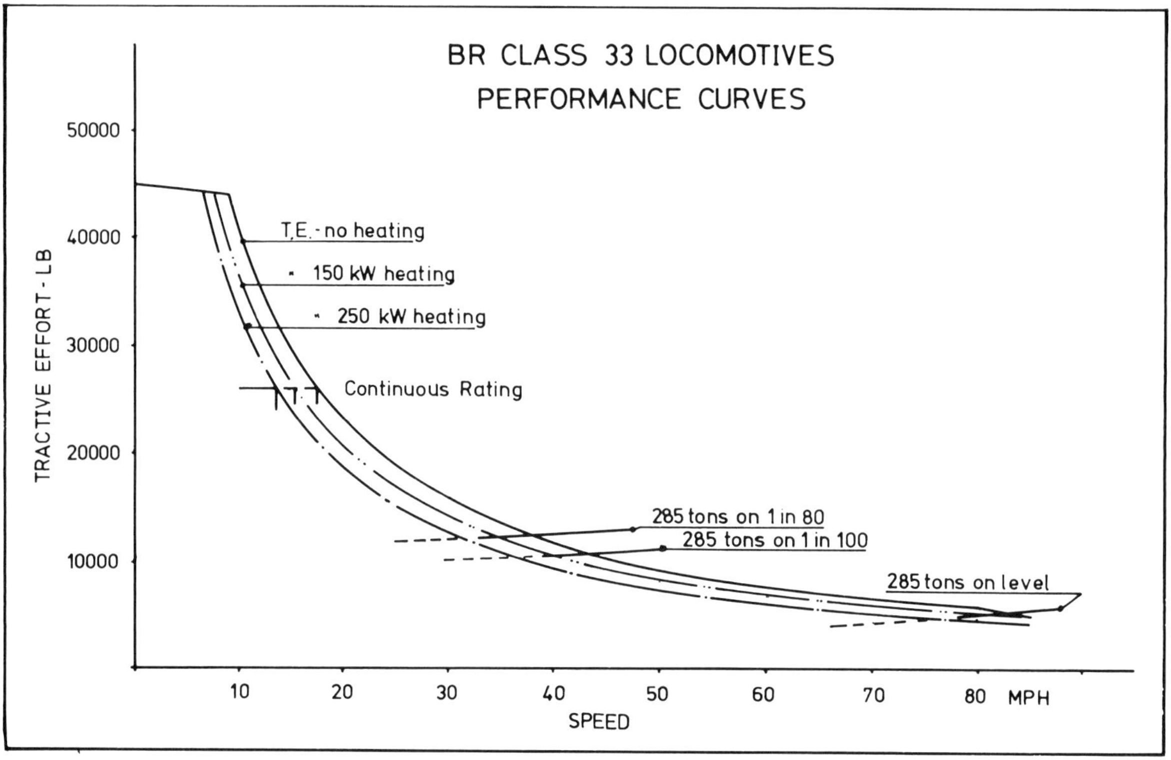
BR CLASS 33 LOCOMOTIVES
PERFORMANCE CURVES
TRACTIVE EFFORT - LB
50000
40000
30000
20000
10000
T.E. - no heating
150 kW heating
250 kW heating
Continuous Rating
285 tons on 1 in 80
285 tons on 1 in 100
285 tons on level
10
20
30
40
50
60
70
80
MPH
SPEED

Fig 22 Class 33 characteristics

case locomotives are still maintained at their home depot, Eastleigh, and changed over on a three-day basis.

Availability of Class 33s has generally been good and the non-steam mentality of the Region's maintenance staff has probably been a contributory factor, coupled with the fact that depots have had far fewer variants with which to contend. One other factor has been the absence of steam generators which have elsewhere been a large factor in loss of availability.

As examples of performance in normal train running, the following tables give some idea of what to expect:

Table I details a typical run on the 'Push-Pull' service from Glasgow to Edinburgh, Haymarket with the then standard 6-coach formation with No 27.201 at the head end of the train and No 27.102 at the rear. These services are now of course operated by the specially fitted Class 47/7 with Mk 3 coaches and a converted Mk 2 driving trailer. The train in question had a tare weight of 192ton, 205ton full, and with the installed power of two Class 27s giving some 7.4bhp/ton of train weight. Now with a Class 47/7 the figure is 8.5bhp/ton of train weight but power for train heating is taken from the main engines to that power for traction is about the equal of the two Class 27s formerly used.

But to return to *Table 1*, Cowlairs was passed in 3min 48sec against the allowance of 4½min and with

Table I: Scottish Region: Glasgow Queen St-Edinburgh Haymarket 15.30 'Push-Pull'

Locomotives: Nos 27.201, 27.102
Load: 6 vehicles; 192 tons tare, 205 tons full

Dist Miles		Sch min	Actual m s	Speeds mph
0.00	QUEEN STREET	0	0 00	—
1.85	*Cowlairs*	4½	3 48	45
3.25	Bishopbriggs		5 19	64
5.00	Cadder		6 58	65
6.25	Lenzie	8½	8 02	75
11.50	Croy		12 05	81
15.50	Castle Cary		15 00	86
17.25	*Greenhill Upper Junc*	16	16 13	83
18.50	Bonnybridge		17 06	88
21.80	FALKIRK HIGH		19 27	72/67*
25.00	Polmont	22	22 13	76
27.25	*Bo'ness Junc*		23 53	84
29.65	Linlithgow	25½	25 37	83
33.00	Philipstoun		28 02	83
34.75	*Winchburgh Junc*	29½	29 18	81
39.50	*Queensferry Junc*		32 43	86
44.00	*Saughton Junc*		35 49	84/pws*
46.10	HAYMARKET	43	39 26	

* Speed restriction. Net time 38min

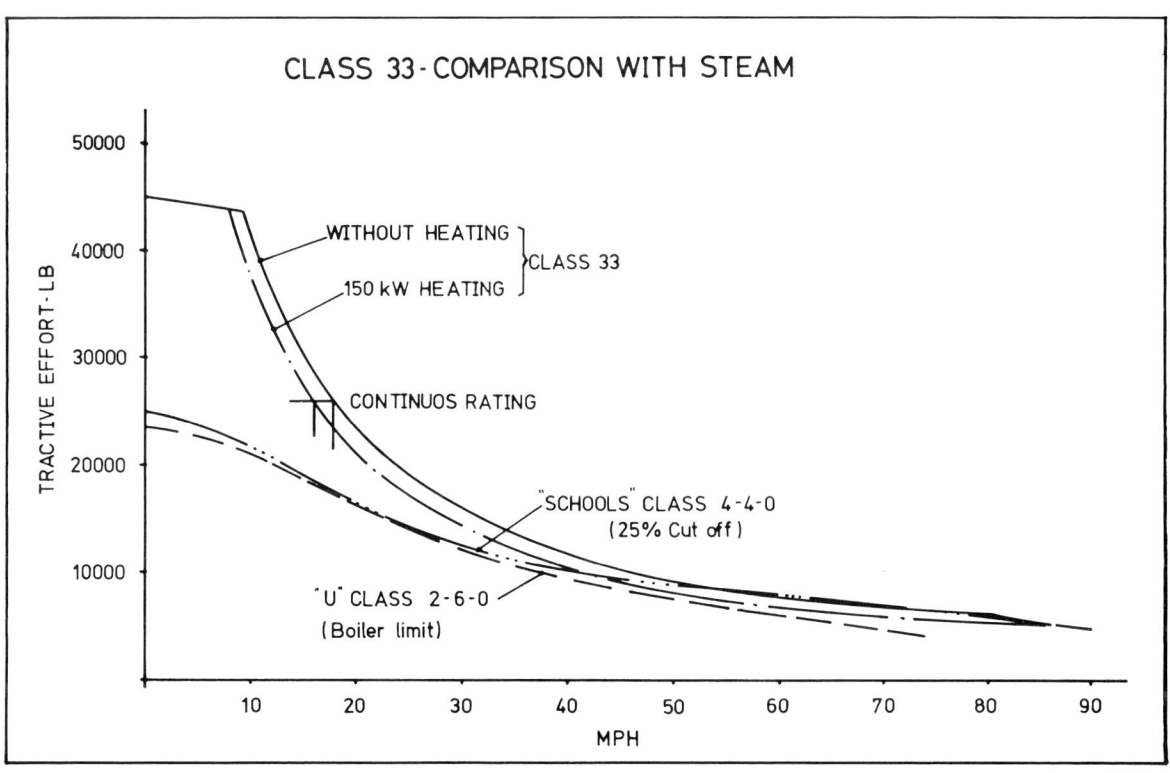

CLASS 33 - COMPARISON WITH STEAM

Fig 23   Class 33 characteristics compared with steam

one minor speed restriction en route and a severe pws after Saughton Junction, Haymarket was reached in 39min 26sec (38min net) against the 43min allowed. Sectional time was just about maintained while the

28.5 miles from Lenzie to Winchburg were covered at an average speed of 80.4mph inclusive of a speed restriction through Falkirk High.

But the earlier and less powerful Class 26 have been used widely throughout the northerly routes from Glasgow and Edinburgh singly and in pairs. *Table II* gives details of a run behind Nos 26.040 and 26.026 with a load of 469ton tare, 500ton gross between Mossend and Perth on the 'Royal Highlander'. This route was familiar ground for Class 26 until recently, together with the section between Aviemore and Inverness which includes the climb over Slochd Summit (see *Table III*) but perhaps more interesting is a record of two Class 26s, numbers unfortunately not noted hauling 580ton tare, 610ton gross on the southbound 'Motorail' negotiating the punishing initial ascent out of Inverness which includes $11\frac{3}{4}$ miles of 1 in 60 continuously, except for $2\frac{1}{2}$ miles at 1 in 70 and only $\frac{3}{4}$-miles downhill across Culloden Viaduct. The run, detailed in *Table IV* typifies the work of the Class 26 on the Inverness route over the 'Hill'. Again, bear in mind there is an installed power of just 3.0bhp/ton of gross train weight. A similar load behind a Class 47 would benefit from 20% more power, albeit on six axles.

To return to Class 27 two runs on the West Highland line are detailed in *Table V* and *VI*, the first between Garelochhead and Fort William with a load of six coaches of 209ton tare, 215ton full, the second from Fort William to Crianlarich with seven coaches of 264ton tare and 280ton full (the West Highland portion of the Sleeper for Euston). Both runs were affected by a long severe temporary speed restriction of 5mph past the site of a derailment north of Spean Bridge.

The work of the Class 24 and 25s on passenger

Table II: Scottish Region: Mossend-Perth

Locomotive Nos		26.040/26.026	
Load, tons (e/f)		469/500	
Dist Miles		*Actual m s*	*Speeds mph*
0.0	MOSSEND	0 00	—
3.0	Coatbridge	4 50	—
9.3	Cumbernauld	12 47	65
		pws	15
14.7	*Greenhill*	—	55
		sigs	15
18.3	LARBERT	26 16	—
20.5	*Alloa Junc*	29 39	57
22.3	*Plean*	31 37	51
	Bannockburn	—	60
26.4	STIRLING	36 12	35*
28.25	*Cornton*	38 21	60
29.3	Bridge of Allan	39 26	63/56
31.3	Dunblane	41 50	44
34.0	*Kinbuck*	45 30	43
37.2	*Greenloaning*	49 07	63
41.35	*Blackford*	52 49	69
43.7	GLENEAGLES	55 06	57
48.4	*Whitemoss*	58 52	82
52.6	*Forteviot*	62 24	66
57.4	*Hilton Junc*	66 52	—
59.4	PERTH	71 02	—

Speed restrictions

Table III: Scottish Region: Aviemore-Inverness

Locomotive Nos		26.040/26.028	
Load, tons (e/f)		469/500	
Dist Miles		*Actual m s*	*Speeds mph*
0.0	AVIEMORE	0 00	—
		—	49
4.7	*Milepost 88*	7 32	40
		—	46
6.7	Carr Bridge	10 06	—
1.5	*Milepost $91\frac{1}{2}$*	3 40	27
3.5	*Milepost $93\frac{1}{2}$*	—	—
5.4	*Slochd*	11 05	35
		pws	20
9.0	Tomatin	16 52	—
		—	67
13.1	Moy	21 25	60
		pws	20
21.45	Culloden Moor	31 18	—
		—	69
25.45	*Millburn Junc*	—	—
28.0	INVERNESS	40 32	—

Table IV: Scottish Region: Inverness-Carr Bridge

Locomotive Nos		Two 26s	
Load, tons (e/f)		580/610	
Dist Miles		*Actual m s*	*Speeds mph*
0.0	INVERNESS	0 00	—
0.55	*Milburn Junc*	2 21	35
3.75	*Milepost $114\frac{1}{4}$*	8 34	23
		sig stop	—
6.55	Culloden Moor	19 30	—
		—	36
10.85	Daviot	29 33	24
12.75	*Milepost $105\frac{1}{4}$*	pws	20
14.9	Moy	38 19	30
		—	53
19.0	Tomatin	44 04	40*
22.6	*Slochd*	51 52	21/72
		sig stop	—
28.0	CARR BRIDGE	60 50	pass

Speed restrictions

54

trains was never particularly spectacular but the following examples give some idea of their capabilities. *Table VII* is an example of a grossly over-loaded run from Dingwall in which No 24.127 was loaded to 250ton full on a timing intended for a maximum of 175ton, consequently time was lost in spite of the fact the 11.9 miles to Garve, with a ruling grade of 1 in 50 to Raven Rock were covered at a start to stop average speed of 27.6mph with a maximum at the summit of 20mph.

Table VIII is included as a piece of nostalgia and details of the running of Nos 24133/24085 on the 'Farewell Class 24' special between Crewe and Holyhead.

The Class 33, although having a close relationship

Table V: Scottish Region:
Garelochhead-Fort William

Load: 6 cars, 209 tons tare, 215 tons full
Locomotive: Class 27 diesel No 27.003

Dist Miles		Actual m s	Speeds mph
0.0	Garelochhead	0 00	—
1.1	*Milepost 10*	2.48	
2.1	*Milepost 11*	4 48	30/25*
5.1	*Milepost 14*	11 00	32
6.3	Glen Douglas	14.05	—
4.4	Arrochar	11 00	—
8.0	Ardlui	18 00	—
1.4	*Milepost 29*	2 58	36
2.4	*Milepost 30*	4 50	32
—		slack	21*
4.4	*Milepost 32*	9 32	30/20*
6.4	*Milepost 34*	14 24	$33\frac{1}{2}$
7.4	*Milepost 35*	16 11	—
8.7	Crianlarich	18 42	—
0.7	*Milepost 37*	1 42	—
2.7	*Milepost 39*	5 34	$31\frac{1}{2}$
4.7	*Milepost 41*	9 30	$31\frac{1}{2}$
5.0	Tyndrum	10 27	—
1.7	*Milepost 43*	3 49	31
7.5	Bridge of Orchy	13 10	—
1.2	*Milepost 50*	2 56	—
3.2	*Milepost 52*	5 16	40
5.2	*Milepost 54*	8 30	—
7.2	*Milepost 56*	11 58	35
8.7	Gortan	14 08	—
12.5	Rannoch	25 48	—
1.8	*Milepost $66\frac{1}{4}$*	5.47	25
7.3	Corrour	13 22	—
10.0	Tulloch	17 05	—
15.7	Roy Bridge	26 17	—
18.7	Spean Bridge	32 17	—
—		pws	5
27.2	Mallaig Junc	50 25	—
28.2	FORT WILLIAM	52 45	—

* Speed restrictions

Table VI: Scottish Region:
Fort William-Crianlarich

Load: 7 cars, 264 tons tare, 280 tons full
Locomotive: Class 27 diesel No 27.038

Dist Miles		Actual m s	Speeds mph
0.0	FORT WILLIAM	0 00	—
1.0	*Mallaig Junc*	1 58	—
2.9	*Milepost 97*	4 40	50 (max)
—		pws	5
6.9	*Milepost 93*	17 47	50
9.5	Spean Bridge	21 10	—
—		pws	22
3.0	Roy Bridge	6 17	—
2.4	*Milepost 85*	5 21	30
—		pws	
5.7	Tulloch	11 09	—
0.7	*Milepost 81*	2 05	29
3.0	*Milepost $78\frac{3}{4}$*	6 36	46
6.7	*Milepost 75*	14 16	29
8.7	*Milepost 73*	18 18	$30\frac{1}{2}$
10.0	*Corrour*	21 00	—
7.3	Rannoch	11 15	—
—		pws	20
6.9	*Gortan*	11 53	50 (max)
15.6	Bridge of Orchy	23 58	—
1.8	*Milepost 47*	4 35	35
—		—	30*
3.8	*Milepost 45*	7 54	28
5.8	*Milepost 43*	12 37	25
7.5	Tyndrum	15 42	—
5.0	Crianlarich	8.55	—

* Speed restriction

Table VII:

Load: 7=233 tons tare, 250 tons full
Locomotive: Class 24 No 24.127
(Normal load limits 175 tons)

Dist Miles		Actual m s	Speed mph
0.00	DINGWALL	0 00	—
2.0	*Milepost 2*	6 01	20*/40
3.0	*Milepost 3*	7 36	30
4.0	*Milepost 4*	10 03	22
—	Achterneed	—	24
6.25	Raven Rock		
	Milepost $6\frac{1}{4}$	16 13	20
9.0	*Milepost 9*	21 06	42 (max)
11.9	Garve	25 50	—
1.1	*Milepost 13*	4 02	20
2.1	Corriemuillie		
	Milepost 14	6 40	25
—		—	53 (max)
5.2	Lochluichart	11 22	—

* Speed restriction

55

Table VIII: 'Farewell 24s' Tour: March, 1976
Load: 10 coaches, 331 tons tare, 350 tons full
Locomotives: 2 Class 24s Nos 24.133/24.085

Dist Miles		Schedule m s	Actual m s	Speed mph
0.0	CREWE	0 00	0 00	—
—		—	Sigs	—
3.2	*Milepost 161¼*		7 00	65/60
8.1	Calverley	—	11 38	67
10.5	Beeston Castle	—	13 46	72
16.2	Tattenhall Junc	17 00	18.32	70
21.1	CHESTER	25 00	26 00	15*
—			Sigs	12
24.3	Molt Junc	31 00	32 28	62
26.9	Sandycroft		34 52	68/70
33.5	Flint		40 49	65
37.8	Holywell Junc	42 00	44 28	72
41.2	Mostyn		47 13	76
44.0	Talacre		49 42	67
47.4	Prestatyn		52 39	72
51.0	RHYL	54 00	55 46	66
55.3	Abergele		59 26	71
59.0	Llysfaen Box		62 41	62
—			sig/stop	—
65.4	LLANDUDNO JC	74 00	77 52	40*
70.8	Penmaenmawr		84 00	59/53*
75.6	Aber Box		88 48	69 (max)
80.8	BANGOR	90 00	93 28	57/59
—	Brittania Bridge		—	15*
—	Gaerwen Box	106.00	106 24	11 sigs
87.1	Bodorgan		113 25	68/55
93.6	Ty Croes		115 56	74/62
102.0	Valley		120 54	68
—			Sigs	—
105.5	HOLYHEAD	131.00	128.18	—

Left: **Waterloo-Salisbury train passing Battledown behind double-headed Class 33s. Note electric MU jumpers and air pipes.** *A. T. H. Tayler*

Right: **Newcastle-Poole train passing Battledown Junction hauled by Class 33/1 No 33.104.** *A. T. H. Tayler*

Below: **No 24.035 with a freight from Mold Junction regaining the main line at Valley, bound for Holyhead, 20 January 1978.** *L. Goddard*

Table IX: Class 33 Waterloo-Exeter, January 1972

Locomotive: No 6544 (33.026) — 8 coaches,
286 tons tare, 295 tons full

Dist Miles		Schedule m s	Actual m s	Speed mph
0.00	WATERLOO	0 00	0 00	—
3.90	Clapham Jc	6 30	6 17	62/42*
7.30	Wimbledon		10 11	60
—			Sigs	22
12.05	Surbiton		15 53	64
13.55	Hampton Court Jc	16 30	17 06	70
19.10	Weybridge		21 38	77
21.65	West Byfleet		23 35	81
24.30	WOKING	26 30	26 18	—
3.70	Brookwood		5 12	60
6.70	*Milepost 31*		8 06	64
8.95	Farnborough		9 59	73
12.20	Fleet		12 36	80
17.90	Hook		16.58	76/77
21.70	*Milepost 46*		19 57	81
23.50	BASINGSTOKE	22 30	22 00	—
4.60	Oakley		6 12	70
7.80	Overton		10 23	Sig stop
			12 42	—
15.30	*Milepost 63*		23 15	spl stop
—			33 52	—
18.55	ANDOVER	19 00	38 52	—
1.65	*Milepost 68*		3 03	53
3.65	*Milepost 70*		5 00	65
5.65	*Milepost 72*		6 53	63
6.90	Grateley ($73\frac{1}{4}$ MP)		8 07	60
11.90	Porton		11 58	90 max
13.50	Tunnel Jc	17	15 20	—
14.60	SALISBURY	20 03	18 45	—
0.00	SALISBURY	0 00	0 00	—
2.50	Wilton South	5 30	4 38	41/31*
8.30	Dinton (92)		11 31	69
12.55	Tisbury ($96\frac{1}{4}$)		15 12	68/72
17.55	Semley ($101\frac{1}{4}$)		19 37	61
20.30	*Milepost 104*		21 45	88
21.55	GILLINGHAM	24 30	23 25	—
2.25	*Milepost $107\frac{1}{2}$*		3 54	46
4.75	*Milepost 110*		6 03	83
6.95	Templecombe Box	8 30	8 04	40*
8.25	*Milepost $113\frac{1}{2}$*		10 19	43
11.75	*Milepost 117*		13 39	77
13.00	SHERBORNE	16 00	15 16	—
2.75	*Milepost 121*		3 59	62
4.60	YEOVIL JC	7 30	7 18	—
3.40	*Milepost $126\frac{1}{4}$*		5 30	50
7.15	*Milepost 130*		8 47	79
10.40	*Milepost $133\frac{1}{4}$*		11 50	61
16.65	Chard Jc ($139\frac{1}{2}$)	23 00	16 47	84/80
19.15	*Milepost 144*		20 11	86
21.95	AXMINSTER	27 00	21 18	—
2.95	Seaton Jc ($147\frac{3}{4}$)		4 27	62/54
7.15	*Milepost 152*		10 28	37
			pws	22
—			15 50 —	
10.15	HONITON	16 30		
3.00	*Milepost 158*		3 42	84
4.60	Feniton		4 41	69 min
11.00	*Milepost 166*		9 56	88
15.70	Exmouth Jc	18 30	13 21	67
16.75	EXETER CENTRAL	21 00	15 30	—

*Speed restriction

Table X: Bournemouth–Weymouth

Locomotive: No 6532 (33.114) hauling 4TC unit
132 tons tare, 140 tons full

Dist Miles		Schedule m s	Actual m s	Speed mph
0.0	BOURNEMOUTH	0 00	0 00	—
2.7	Branksome		3 55	50 (max)
5.8	POOLE	9 00	7 58	—
2.2	Hamworthy Jc		3 31	30*
5.0	Holton Heath		6 21	72
7.1	WAREHAM	10 00	8 45	—
1.1	Worgret Jc		1 59	
—			—	72 (max)
5.0	WOOL	8 00	6 10	—
4.5	Moreton		4 56	69
—			—	55*
—			—	73
10.0	DORCHESTER	12 00	10 39	—
1.3	Monkton Halt		2 13	56
2.6	Bincombe Tunnel Box		3 38	55
3.4	Upwey Wishing Well Halt		4 21	—
4.6	Upwey		5 16	76½
5.9	Radipole		6 34	—
—			Sigs	—
7.0	Weymouth	10 30	9.30	—

* *Speed restriction*

Table XI: Weymouth–Bournemouth

Locomotive: No 6532 (33.114) propelling 4TC
132 tons tare, 140 tons full

Dist Miles		Schedule m s	Actual m s	Speed mph
0.00	Weymouth	0 00	0.00	—
1.1	Radipole		1 52	54—
2.4	Upwey		3 17	53½
3.6	Upwey Wishing Well Halt		4 39	50½
4.4	Bincombe Tunnel Box		5 40	45
5.7	Monkton Halt		6 44	75
6.6	Dorchester Jc	12 30	8 15	—
7.1	DORCHESTER	15 30	10 35	—
5.5	Moreton		5 20	80½ (max)
10.0	Wool	10 30	9 25	—
3.9	Worgret Jc	4 00	4 20	72 (max)
5.0	WAREHAM	7 30	6 14	—
1.9	Holton Heath		2 40	76 (max)
4.9	Hamworthy Jc		5 20	35*
7.1	POOLE	10 00	9 10	—
1.8	Parkstone		2 40	52½/50½
3.1	Branksome		4 24	30*
5.8	BOURNEMOUTH	10 30	8 25	—

* *Speed restriction*

Above left: **Pre-electrification Euston, evening rush hour suburban trains, No D5020 departing and No D5019 awaiting right of way.**

Left: **The 16.30 Edinburgh-Glasgow passing Bo'ness Junction sandwiched between two Class 27/2s.** *G. A. Watt*

with Class 26/27 is, by virtue of its geographical operating area, employed more as a true mixed traffic unit. In its time it has worked more main-line passenger miles probably than its counterparts and to good purpose. Their heyday on the Waterloo-Exeter services is now over but it is appropriate to include one log on that service.

Table IX sets out a run from Waterloo to Exeter Central on the day in January 1972 when the train was badly delayed near Whitchurch while the Driver and Guard removed a small tree which had blown over and was suspended foul of the down line. Once away again the crews and station staff set to and recouped all of the lost time, nearly 20min at Andover, and finally reached Exeter Central just 2min *early*. Fortunately the single line sections between Salisbury and Exeter were all clear and, but for a pw slack approaching Honiton, even better times would have been achieved.

As it was from Andover to Exeter except for the Sherborne-Yeovil Junction and Axminster to Honiton Sections (for the reasons given above), all of the actual

Wirral Railway Circle railtour, the 'Hebridean' photographed at Garve. Class 24/1 Nos D5126 and D5130.

times were within the current sectional times for Class 50 haulage, and the maximum permitted speed of 85mph for the class was exceeded only at three points and then by no more than 3 to 5mph, with $13\frac{1}{2}$min being regained by the locomotive.

The other passenger duty regularly performed by Class 33s since the inception of the Bournemouth electrification in 1967 is the hourly push-pull service of the Weymouth portion of the London trains between Bournemouth and Weymouth. These are of course operated by the '33/1s', hauling a 4TC set, sometimes two, to Weymouth and propelling on the return. Two logs are reproduced as *Tables X* and *XI*.

The 35 miles from Bournemouth, allowed 52min with four intermediate stops incorporates a drop to sea level at Poole, a gentle rise to Wool followed by a stiff climb to Moreton. After Dorchester there is a climb of 1 in 91 to Bincombe Tunnel and then a sharp drop of 1 in 50/60 past Upwey to Weymouth. The return trip therefore has the formidable climb to the north end of Bincombe Tunnel, in the case quoted, passed at 45mph. At the other end of the line the climb at 1 in 60 from Poole was negotiated at a minimum of $50\frac{1}{2}$mph. In this run, with four coaches, the schedule was cut by 10min. With eight coaches, of course time would be kept, but with little in hand.

7 Brake Equipment

Brakes on British Railways, except for electric multiple-unit stock and certain 'odd-balls' eg LNER Great Eastern suburban services and the Isle of Wight, were vacuum orientated. At modernisation in 1953 the then Railway Executive nearly made the change to air, but finally decided to continue with vacuum.

At a meeting on 8 December 1955, the Technical Development and Research Committee agreed on a recommendation to a change to automatic air brakes at an estimated cost of £30million. The Regional General Managers then convened a separate meeting where they expressed their deep concern over the serious disturbance to operation which would occur during the period when vacuum and air braked trains would be running over the system at the same time. The Southern Region was the one region prepared to go along with the air brakes decision. On 16 February 1956 the Commission ruled the vacuum brake should

be adopted as the standard system on British Railways. (See *The Modernisation of British Railways 1948-80* by Johnson & Long. Mechanical Engineering Publications Ltd).

The pioneers, Nos 10000/1 and 10800, all had vacuum brakes while Nos 10201-3 had a vacuum controlled straight air brake with independent air brake valves to apply the locomotive brake independently of the train. The latter gave a vastly superior performance, especially when unfitted or partially fitted freight trains had to be operated, as was very frequently the case in the 1950s.

The decision, although not conceded in such a blunt way at the time, was evidently the wrong one, except for the of short-term operational benefit. Subsequent events later confirmed that it was wrong in engineering and operating terms as some of the operating practices of today would not have been practical

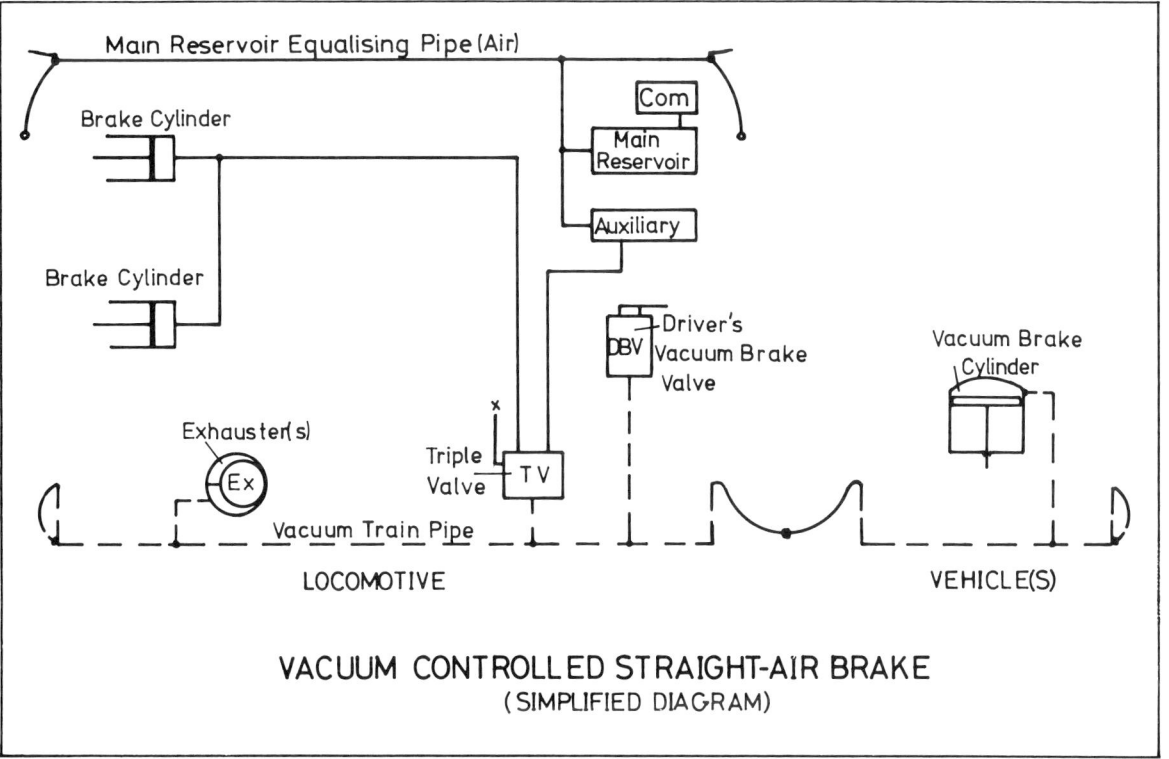

Fig 24 Vacuum controlled straight air brake

Above: **Vacuum exhauster and additional air compressor and part of 'brake frame' on a Class 25.** *Stewart Bale Ltd*

Right: **View of engine room on Class 26/0 showing neat arrangement of air compressor and exhauster.**

without air braking. Ten years were to go by before the decision taken in 1956 was reserved.

Nevertheless, for good engineering reasons the straight air brake with vacuum control was specified for all diesel and electric locomotives under the modernisation scheme. Powerful air brakes could be accommodated with bogie mounted cylinders and the minimum of mechanical connections between under-frame and bogies.

In the case of the locomotives described in this book, the standard brake specification applied, except for the Class 33, the reasons for which have been mentioned already. As built all of the Type 2s (Classes 24, 25, 26, 27) had vacuum controlled straight air brakes, supplied either by Westinghouse of Chippen-ham or Davies & Metcalfe of Romilly, Cheshire. The latter was, at that time, a relative newcomer to the British Railways scene but had concluded a license agreement with the Oerlikon Engineering Company of Switzerland to manufacture and develop their brake equipment in the United Kingdom, already accepted and approved by the UIC.

Classes 24 and 25 had a direct air brake on the locomotive in which air is supplied from the main air reservoir and regulated by the driver's straight air brake valve to relay valves. The relay valves handle a much larger quantity of air than the driver's brake valve, which acts as a control to regulate the air pressure supplied through the relay valves to the bogie-mounted brake cylinders. Air pressure in the cylinders is proportional to the angular movement of the driver's air brake valve. This valve is used for light locomotive movements or when hauling unfitted trains. It can also be used to apply the air brake on the locomotive independently of the train.

Air was supplied by either a Davies & Metcalfe 2A115 motor driven air compressor or a Westinghouse DVC2 compressor. Air required for other services, eg steam generator, electrical control gear, windscreen wipers, horns, etc is also taken from the main air reservoir.

Vacuum train braking equipment was provided to control both train and locomotive brakes in sympathy. Two Westinghouse 4V110 or two Reavell FRU $5\frac{1}{4}$in $\times$ 10in exhausters created vacuum in a continuous train pipe. Operation of the driver's vacuum brake valve regulates the vacuum in the train pipe, which in turn operates a 'triple valve' which in turn controls the air to the brake cylinders from an anciliary reservoir in direct proportion to the vacuum brake on the train.

On Classes 24 and 25 the majority of brake equipment was mounted on a frame at the free (non-generator) end of the engine above the compressor, while on the BRCW-built locomotives Classes 26 and 27 the various brake valves were disposed mainly under the cab desks. The exhausters were mounted in similar positions to the Classes 24 and 25, in the radiator tunnel, while the air compressor was at the right-hand end of the engine room.

When it became clear that a change from vacuum to air braking was inevitable a decision had to be made as to which locomotives had to be immediately modified and which could be left as they were. Some types of vehicle would remain vacuum-braked and some, mainly new vehicles, would be air-braked. Therefore automatic air brake equipment would have to be added leaving conversions still able to work vacuum braked trains.

But let us now look at the BRCW Type 3 (Class 33). In spite of the BTC decision, the Southern Region had insisted upon the provision of locomotives with automatic air brakes for the very good reason that by far the largest proportion of its trains already had air brakes and the deal was finally clinched when it was pointed out to the BTC that on a fully electrified railway an area power failure would mean diesel locomotives having to haul passenger trains loose-coupled and with a severe speed limitation unless the locomotives were compatible.

The system adopted for the Class 33 was similar to that already applied to the Region's Bo-Bo electric locomotives. In this case the whole system was supplied by Davies & Metcalfe. The Oerlikon automatic air system was already well-established on the continent of Europe and for this application needed some additional control elements to control vacuum train brakes. Whereas in the vacuum controlled system the separate vacuum brake valve controls the locomotive brake through a proportional valve. In the Class 33 system it is the automatic driver's air brake valve which controls the admission of air to the vacuum train pipe, in turn applying the locomotive air

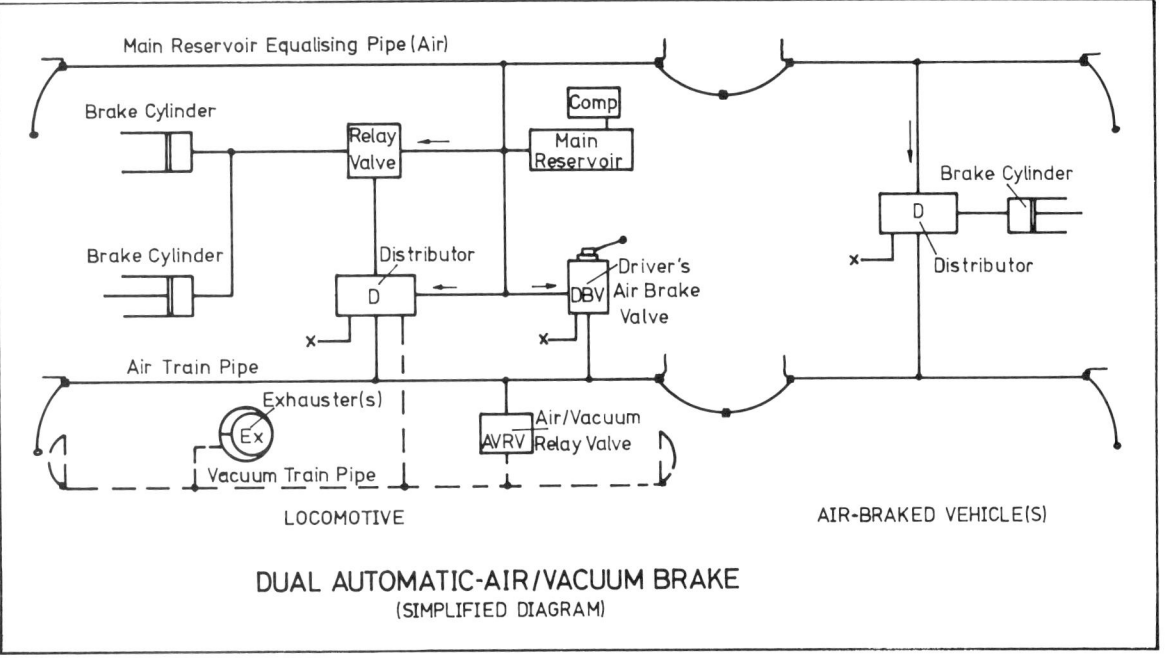

DUAL AUTOMATIC-AIR/VACUUM BRAKE
(SIMPLIFIED DIAGRAM)

Fig 25   Dual auto-air/vacuum brake

brakes in proportion. The mode of operation is selected by whether or not the vacuum exhausters are running.

The Class 33 locomotives have one Metcalfe/Oerlikon 3A115 motor-driven air compressor mounted across-wise at the generator end and two Reavell FRU $5\frac{1}{4}$in $\times$ 10in rotary exhausters, only one of which runs to maintain train pipe vacuum while both are brought in at a high speed to obtain a quick release.

Unlike other British Railways locomotives, controls are duplicated either side of each cab, the offside controls being operated from the master brake valves through Teleflex controls.

In effect, what has now become the BR automatic brake systen is a two-pipe system, that is each vehicle has two pipes, an automatic air brake or train pipe, normally charged to 70psi when brakes are released, and a main reservoir equalising or charging pipe making the system virtually inexhaustible. Viewing a locomotive from the front there are 10 connections as follows:

1 Engine air control pipe.
2 Train heating supply socket.
3 Main reservoir equalising pipe.
4 Control coupler socket.
5 Vacuum train pipe.
6 Automatic air train brake pipe.
7 Control coupler socket (duplicate — only one has to be used).
8 Main reservoir equalising pipe (duplicate).
9 Train heating jumper (positive) cable and plug (housed in dummy).
10 Engine air control pipe (duplicate).

The photograph shows the standard layout of connections on a Class 33/0. For push-pull operation the Class 33/1 has a drop-head buckeye coupler and waist-level air (main reservoir and train) pipes, plus electric multiple-unit control jumper and socket.

Following the introduction of air braking, selected locomotives have been converted. No Class 24s received auto-air braking as might have been expected. Some 110 Class 25/1 locomotives were converted to a system similar to that on Class 33, together with seven Class 26/0 and 36 Class 27/0, while all of the 'Edinburgh-Glasgow' batch, Classes 27/1 and 27/2, were similarly fitted.

Vacuum–controlled straight air brake (Fig 24)

Initially fitted to Classes 24, 25, 26, 27. Requires vacuum exhauster(s) to run continuously to create a vacuum of 21in/hg (mercury) in the vacuum train pipe (VTP).

Brake is applied by movement of driver's vacuum brake valve (DBV) which admits atmospheric air to the VTP applying brakes on train vehicles — vacuum brake cylinder piston moves downwards. Simultaneously the triple valve is operated by the reduction in TP vacuum and allows air to flow from the auxiliary reservoir to the locomotive brake cylinders in proportion to the drop in TP vacuum. Release of the brakes is by returning the DBV handle to the release or running position when TP vacuum is restored to normal and the triple valve releases the air from the locomotive brake cylinders to atmosphere.

An independent brake is also provided on all locomotives which employs a separate simple brake valve (not shown) whose function is to supply air direct to the brake cylinders without affecting the train pipe vacuum. By that means a train can be held at a signal say, with the vacuum brake on the vehicles fully released, the locomotive holding the complete train ready for an immediate start.

Dual automatic — air vacuum brake (Fig 25)

Fitted originally to the whole of Class 33 — now added to some of Class 25, 26 and 27. Enables air or vacuum braked stock to be operated. Vacuum exhausters need only to be running when hauling vacuum braked trains. The air brake is known as a

'two-pipe system' because it employs the air main reservoir equalising pipe which charges and equalises the auxiliary reservoirs on the vehicles forming the train and air train pipe — the control pipe — which is normally fed through the operating driver's automatic air brake valve (DBV) and maintained at 70lb/sq in.

Brake is applied by movement of driver's brake valve to reduce the train pipe pressure to any value between 70 and 48lb/sq in (the full brake application control pressure). The pressure reduction causes the distributor (D) to send an air pressure signal to the relay valve (RV) which in turn allows air at a controlled pressure to flow from the main reservoirs to the locomotive brake cylinders. Similarly on the train vehicles,

the brakes are applied by the drop in the train pipe pressure, but in this case the brake cylinders are fed from auxiliary reservoirs on each vehicle. These are the reservoirs referred to above.

When hauling vacuum braked stock the driver's air brake valve still controls the pressure in the (locomotive) air train pipe but now the exhausters are running to create a vacuum in the VTP. Movement of the driver's air brake valve operates the air/vacuum relay valve (AVRV) which in turn regulates the degree of vacuum in the VTP and by means of a vacuum-operated portion of the distributor, the locomotive air brakes in proportion.

An independent straight air brake is also provided.

Top: **Clapham Junction-Eastleigh parcels passing Battledown behind No 33.007, March 1982.** *A. T. H. Tayler*

Above: **Class 24 No 5134 seen leaving Norton Colliery, 8 December 1973.** *C. Plant*

8 Chronological Survey

The previous chapters have dealt with the technical aspects and it is now appropriate to make a survey of the five classes and to bring out some of the more important landmarks in their respective 'lives', already briefly mentioned in previous chapters, highlighting changes in utilisation, modifications and indeed their development generally.

Classes 24 and 25

The first official appearance of No D5000 was at Marylebone on 24 July 1958 when it was formally inspected by the late General Sir Brian Robertson, the then chairman of the British Transport Commission, and other members of the Commission. It was afterwards returned to Derby and was officially taken into stock in August 1958. At that time, pilot scheme not withstanding, a total of 114 had been ordered!

Although declared in publicity at the time as being of 75ton in working order, the real weight was 79.8ton, which led to the Southern Region civil engineers imposing severe route restrictions, effectively barring them from the London area until the boilers were removed from Nos 5002-6, giving a wider availability for them but leaving Nos D5000/1/7-14 in the East Kent area. Nor were they allowed to run coupled, to each other or to anything else!

No D5008 was returned to the LMR in June 1959 in exchange for No D5017, to undergo dynamometer car tests. The reason for the selection of No D5008 is not now clear! At the same time the SR Civil Engineer lifted his embargo — some bridge strengthening had been completed — and pairs were rostered for working the Margate-Birkenhead train to and from Redhill. Derby's first batch of 30 was completed as a further batch began to emerge from Crewe and by 12 January 1960 Darlington Works had also turned out its first, No D5094.

In October 1960, Nos D5116/24/6/8/9 visited St Rollox Works, Glasgow, to have tablet catchers fitted to enable them to work on the Highland Line. But introduction to the Highland line was slow and with some reluctance because experience since April of that year had not been good with a reputation for unreliability, cold draughty cabs and a layout inferior to the BRCW Type 2, while performance, even in pairs on the Perth-Inverness passenger trains, left a lot to be desired, even though on freight workings they could take heavier loads than the Class 5 4-6-0s.

No D5133 was the first Type 2 to carry the then new four-character train indicator boxes which came into operation officially on 2 January 1961, while the last 1,160hp, Type 2 (Class 24) No D5150 was completed by Derby in February 1961 and was allocated to Gateshead in the former North Eastern Region.

The first Class 24 to receive an intermediate overhaul was No D5007 at Eastleigh in March/April 1960 and subsequently all of the Southern Region allocation passed through Eastleigh Works before being returned to the LMR. One problem giving rise to some concern was rather high piston ring wear, while in service there had been cooling water leakage from cylinder liners. Initially, locomotives were returned to the SE Division on Boat Trains but some proved too heavy for timekeeping and later the Southampton Old Docks-Nine Elms freights were worked

Stratford Works undertook overhaul of the Eastern Region allocation in 1962 and until closure at the end of 1963, while others were undertaken at Darlington and, of course, Derby.

The great freeze-up of January 1963 took its toll of Type 2s and many, particularly on the LMR, suffered frozen engine blocks, radiators, pipes, etc. The Euston suburban services were particularly badly affected by shortage of motive power.

Early in 1964 the Tyne Dock-Consett Iron Ore trains were taken over by pairs of Type 2s in multiple. Nos D5102-11 were fitted with an extra air compressor in the boiler compartment and controls for operating the wagon doors. Banking assistance on the 1 in 35/51 grades was not provided with two locomotives in multiple.

Going back a little in time, the first up-rated Type 2 No D5151 left Darlington Works on 15 April 1961 and was allocated to Thornaby. The chief change was the employment of the 6LDA28-B engine rated at 1,250bhp, 750rpm and a change of traction motor gear ratio to give a top speed of 90mph. Otherwise they employed the same equipment as the earlier Class 24s. From No D5176 (25.026) the smaller, lighter AEI 253 traction motor was employed as standard.

A further, more obvious change occurred in late 1963 with No D5233 (25.083) when a body style, more akin to the BRCW design, was adopted but without nose-end doors, together with a painting style similar to that used on the Class 47. The original BR

design had always suffered from the ingress of dirt, particularly from brake blocks, due to the low position of some of the air intakes. Apart from a dirty engine/equipment compartment, piston ring and cylinder liner wear was also higher than in the corresponding BRCW types.

In July 1965, No D7624 (25.274) was turned out by Beyer Peacock, Gorton, the first of 36 built by the only outside contractor to build to a BR design.

No D7660 was for a time an oddity. The first of a batch of Derby-built Type 2s to be fitted with air brakes, it was turned out in blue, receiving one set of numbers below the cab windows at one end and another set of numbers to the rear of the cab doors at the other end. Subsequently other members of the class had both sets of numbers to the rear of the cab doors and the double-arrow totem below the cab windows.

Blue livery was applied to both Classes 24 and 25 from the early part of 1967 following main Works overhaul, the blue being applied over the roof as well as sides and ends.

The final member of Class 25 was No D7677 (25.327), turned out from Derby Works in May 1967. There was then a total of 478 locomotives built to BR design, 151 of Class 24 (1,160hp) and 327 of Class 25 (1,250hp), although the actual classification did not take place until 1968. With the final demise of steam in 1968 the 'D'-prefix was dropped until renumbering in the 24xxx and 25xxx series which commenced in 1973.

In September 1967 Nos D5127/31 were fitted experimentally with headlights to give approach warning to users of unprotected level crossings. From about this time also some rationalisation of locomotive allocations began to emerge and gradually all of Classes 24 and 25 were dispersed from the Eastern Region to the LM and Scottish Regions and later some to the Western Region.

An interesting incident occurred in the latter part of 1969 when in November of that year a landslide occurred between Strathcarron and Kyle of Lochalsh which severed the line and No D5125 was stranded, together with some coaches. For almost eight weeks No D5125 maintained a service between Kyle and the landslip until relieved by another Class 24 on 5 January 1970. The changeover was made by the operation of No D5125 propelling a rake of wagons past the landslide, shutting down the engine and the whole assembly was then slowly pulled past by the relieving locomotive. The process was reversed to get the relief on to the Kyle side of the slip when it worked the service until 4 March 1970, when repairs were completed.

Another marooning occurred when the Menai Bridge was damaged by fire on 4 May 1970. Nos D5034/44/83 were at Holyhead and were finally rescued by sea and taken to Barrow-in-Furness in July 1970.

Both classes have been involved in collisions, derailments, etc. The first serious accident to a Class 24 occurred on 10 November 1959 at Faversham when No D5000, hauling an unfitted coal train from Snowdown Colliery ran away on the 1 in 110 down gradient and ended up in the sand-drag at the London end of the station with its rear cab in the air and foul of the main line, having completely demolished the buffer stops. Damage was considerable but No D5000 was rescued, towed to Derby Works and repaired.

Two Class 25s were involved in a collision near Flitwick on 10 February 1966 when No D5218 hauling 12 loaded wagons and a brake van crashed into No D7573 standing on the down slow line. Both were towed to Bedford shed and later despatched for repair to Derby Works. But on 9 September 1968, No D5122 ran into the back of a DMU at Castlecary, being damaged so badly it was subsequently withdrawn and scrapped.

However, probably the most devastating accident

Left: **No D6502 on acceptance test run near St Mary Cray Junction, March 1960.** *BR*

Right: **Nos D6506, 20001 and E5005 at Three Bridges for track loading trials, 17 July 1960.** *A. T. H. Tayler*

Below: **Nos D6533 and D6580 at Fawley, marshalling a 'Superline' tank car train.** *Morgan-Wells*

occurred at Chester on 9 July 1969, when Class 47, No 1617, hauling a 1,000ton ore train ran out of control and was switched on to a line leading to the diesel depot, where it crashed into Nos D5031/43/93, D5138/9. Damage was so severe that all except No D5031 were withdrawn.

The first Class 25 casualty to be withdrawn was No D5278 which was taken out of stock in May 1971, following a collision. The first Class 24 withdrawal was No 5051 in 1967 and No 5122 went in 1968, both due to uneconomic repairs. Due to a downturn in demand for the smaller locomotives nine of the earlier Class 24s were withdrawn from stock in January 1969. No D5000 was first followed by Nos D5001/5/10/9. Officially the reason was that 'expensive work was becoming necessary and they did not incorporate certain improvements applied from No D5030 onwards'. No D5010 was, however, reinstated in May

1969, Nos D5011/6/7 were also stored for a time, but returned to traffic in July 1969. But due to shortages elsewhere Nos D5000/1/19 were reinstated in October 1959 and, together with No D5013, were sent to the Eastern Region, remaining operational for another six years!

With electrification, changing traffic patterns, the virtual abandoning of wagon-load traffic and the introduction of HST, the need for smaller locomotives has been considerably reduced. Mass withdrawal of Class 24s began in 1975 and by December of that year the number remaining in service was 91. Another 80 were withdrawn in 1976, leaving only 12 in service, one of which, 24.073, had been withdrawn by the Scottish Region in February 1976, but was retained and used by the LMR from Crewe until the latter part of 1978! Two went in 1977; six in 1978 and two in 1979, leaving No 24.081 as the sole survivor until its final demise in October 1980.

Three Class 24s remain on BR, No 97201, ex-RDB968007 (D5061) and named *Experiment* in 1980, while TDB 968008/9 (ex-24.054/142), are used as train heating generators at Newton Abbot and Reading, respectively. In addition, No 5032 is employed for traction on the North Yorkshire Moors Railway and could be said to be privately 'preserved'.

Meanwhile the Class 25s soldier on — in ever reducing numbers, because the pace of withdrawals increased after the demise of the Class 24s. Nevertheless, Class 25s have in their time carried out a number of important assignments, including Royal Train working, where they have almost invariably been used in pairs. For example, an early Royal Train working was on 9 May 1968 when No D5223/6 hauled a special from St Pancras to Nottingham returning the train to Windsor via Banbury on 10 May, and there have been a number of other 'Royal' duties, chiefly on the LMR.

While no Class 24s had dual air/vacuum brakes, a number of Class 25s were so fitted, some, as already mentioned, being so built new, but in all 110 received dual brakes, between 1973 and 1979. All remain in service at the time of writing.

Renumbering commenced in September 1973 and Nos 5299, 7519, 7558, 7632 became 25.149, 25.169, 25.208 and 25.282 respectively, while in January the class was sub-classified as follows:

25.001-25	25/0	(ex-D5151-75)
25.026-82	25/1	(ex-D5176-232)
25.033-247	25/2	(ex-D5233-99, 7500-7597)
25.248-327	25/3	(ex-7598-7677)

In 1970/71, due to the demise of the Class 22 diesel-hydraulics, a batch of six Class 25s was transferred to the Western Region for use on the Welsh Valley coal trains and in October of 1971 a further batch was transferred from the LM Region. Later, pairs in multiple were used on Port Talbot-Llanwern iron ore trains. Never very popular in South Wales, they were gradually replaced by Class 37s and most gravitated

to Laira for the Cornish China Clay traffic, the last being transferred back to the LM Region towards the end of 1980.

Two of the class made appearances at the Rainhill celebrations in 1980 — Nos 25.144 and 25.296 — both in immaculate condition.

Large withdrawals from service commenced in 1980, by which time their number had been reduced from 327 to 301. By the end of 1981 the class numbered 205 with further withdrawals planned.

Classes 26 and 27

No D5300 was delivered from Smethwick in August 1958 and taken into stock that same month. After acceptance trials in the Doncaster area it was allocated to Hornsey (34B). All 20 of the first 'pilot scheme' batch were originally intended for use on the Great Northern Line, suburban services to Hitchin and Hertford North, replacing the 'N2' and 'L1' class tank engines.

Not so much overweight as the Derby-built Type 2s, the weight was, however, $4\frac{1}{2}$ tons over the original estimate at 77.5 tons and they were consequently barred from working on to the Southern Region via the Metropolitan widened lines.

By March 1959 all 20 had been delivered but by that time the BRCW company had received orders for a further 27, intended for the Scottish Region. Due to problems with other makes, notably the NBL Type 2s, the first six of the next batch also went to Hornsey and each of the first 20 was returned to the BRCW for bogie modifications and some to have pistons changed. Later they were all allocated to the Scottish Region.

On 18 January 1960 a test run was made between Edinburgh and Aberdeen on a 3-hour schedule. Nos D5337/8 hauled an 11-coach load of 350 tons tare weight. A regular daily run was subsequently made and a regular service then commenced. Maintenance facilities at Haymarket were not ready and initially maintenance was carried out at Leith Central — a rather inconvenient arrangement. Eight pairs of Type 2s were diagrammed daily for the Edinburgh-Aberdeen service and a further three pairs worked between Glasgow and Aberdeen.

Prior to the Aberdeen services the BRCW Type 2s had made their mark on the Highland line freight services and by the time that all 47 had been drafted to the Region they had become popular with crews and operators generally, setting the scene for the future.

When further locomotives were required it was natural that a repeat should be called for. The second series was to benefit by the more powerful 6LDA28-B engine but, due to lack of capacity at Cromptons, the electrical equipment was provided by GEC which, in retrospect, was probably a mistake, as possible standardisation was marred by totally different electrical equipment, leading to maintenance difficulties. In all 69 were ordered.

The Scottish Region received the first 23, Nos

D5347-69, the NE Region the next nine, Nos D5370-8, and the remaining 38 went to the LM Region, Nos D5379-5415, to the Midland lines operating from Cricklewood. The NE allocation had no boilers, being intended for freight train operation from Thornaby working mainly on East Coast freight, in pairs, while the LM allocation worked a wide variety of turns from empty stock in and out of St Pancras to main line turns to Nottingham and 'Condor' container trains.

Eventually a more rational allocation of locomotive types was adopted and all of the BRCW Type 2s had gravitated to Scotland by 1970, where they have been the mainstay of the Highland and West Highland lines and have earned a good reputation for reliability.

In 1966 it was decided to adopt Merry-go-round operation at Cockenzie power station and Nos D5300-6 were modified. Slow-speed control and air brakes fitted, and the boilers and end gangways removed, the gangway doors being replaced by steel plates welded over the original openings.

In the BR reclassification of 1968 the 1,160hp locomotives became Class 26 and the 1,250hp loco-motives, Class 27, while the 'D' prefix to the running numbers was dropped. Sub classes were created for Class 26 as follows:

26.001-20   26/0   (ex-5300-19)
26.021-47   26/1   (ex-5320-46)

The first Class 26s to receive new numbers were Nos 26.033, 26.036, 26.040 (ex-5333, 5336, 5340 respectively) in the latter part of 1973. In 1976 fitting of headlights was commenced with No 26.039 and these are now carried by the majority of locomotives.

As with other types, there have been losses due to accidents. On 5 November 1973, there was a collision at Dingwall involving No 5330 which failed to stop at Dingwall North Junction outer home, running into No 5329 waiting to depart to Kyle of Lochalsh, badly damaging both locomotives, although both were later repaired.

To date only six locomotives of Class 26 have been withdrawn and it is now the intention to give a heavy general overhaul to those remaining. To that end, No 26.013 spent an extended period at Crewe Works in 1980 to make an assessment of the work it would be necessary to carry out.

While the Class 27s generally covered similar duties in Scotland, it became necessary in 1970 to improve the Edinburgh-Glasgow services. The 1957 Swindon-built diesel-mechanical sets were becoming obsolescent and requiring expensive repairs. With completion of the motorway, increasing road compe-tition meant something had to be done to improve the rail services. After investigating several possibilities, it was decided to employ an initial multiple-unit forma-tion with a locomotive either end of a rake of six Mk II coaches.

24 Class 27 locomotives were to be adapted to

provide electric train heating and the required number were selected, overhauled, modified; 12 with steam heating and 12 with electric heating from auxiliary alternator sets. Trial running took place between Edin-burgh and Glasgow in April 1971, by which time only seven locomotives were available.

The first recorded re-numbering was No 27.119 (ex-5391) in June 1973. Sub-classes were created in 1974 as follows:

27/0   27.001-44
27/1   27.101-12
27/2   27.201-12

On 31 August 1973 a bridge span at Drimsallie Lodge between Locheilside and Glenfinnan collapsed into the Dubh Lighe river during a flood, trapping Nos 5350 and 5359, plus a quantity of rolling stock on the Mallaig side. For two months the locomotives maintained a shuttle service between Mallaig and the 'break', being supplied with fuel by road. The line was re-joined on 1 November, when Nos 5350/9 were sent to Glasgow for 'maintenance'.

By the end of 1981 the original class of 69 had been reduced to 56. It is the intention to carry out a heavy general overhaul on about half that number, but a final decision is yet to be made.

Class 33

As mentioned in Chapter 1, No D6500 was delivered to the Southern Region on 17 December 1959. Although not officially taken into stock until January 1960, it ran trials from Hither Green a few days later.

Following delivery, each locomotive ran acceptance trials on eight- or 10-coach trains on a round trip Hither Green, Tonbridge, Dover, Canterbury, Favers-ham, Chatham, Dartford, Hither Green, or vice versa.

Due to the experience gained on the Type 2s, BRCW had very carefully calculated their weights and the weight in working order came out at 73.5 tons, well within the original estimate. In consequence the Regional Civil Engineer granted almost universal acceptance throughout the Region, only seven minor branches being barred, plus the Tonbridge-Battle line.

In order to compare the affects of the nose-suspended and fully suspended traction motors on the track, No D6506 was used on special tests over a test site near Balcombe Tunnel Junction, on the Brighton Line, where the Research Department had installed load-measuring baseplates. No D6506 ran coupled to Nos E5004 and 20001. In each direction the leading locomotive hauled the other two.

Initially freight trains on the SE Division were operated as there was only a limited number of passenger vehicles equipped with electric train heating. Later winter steam services were operated in multiple with a Derby Type 2 as train locomotive, to provide steam heat.

In February 1961, No D6504 was employed by Derby on train heating trials with electrically heated

BR Mk 1 vehicles, first on static tests at Derby and then hauling an eight-coach formation between Ferme Park (Hornsey) and Craigentinny (Edinburgh). A photograph reproduced on page 52 shows No D6504 and seven of the eight coaches on arrival at Hornsey from Derby on 10 February. The eighth vehicle came from the Southern Region later the same day.

The complete train ran north on 14 and 16 February, leaving King's Cross at 00.30, due Edinburgh 09.11, returning on 15 and 17 February, leaving Craigentinny at 00.10 due Hornsey 09.30. On those schedules arrival was usually well over one hour ahead of the booked times!

Deliveries continued apace and the last of the 'standard' locomotives was delivered in January 1962, with the first of the 'Hastings' batch arriving in February. The narrow-body was immediately apparent and it was not long before they were dubbed 'Slimlines'. The order was completed in May 1962. Use quickly embraced most of the lines in Kent and Sussex and in April 1962 No D6503 was sent to Eastleigh for driver training in preparation for a batch to be allocated to work the Fawley oil trains. In the latter part of April it was tried on oil trains between Fawley and Didcot, successfully replacing a Class 9 2-10-0 between Eastleigh and Didcot, the first diesel operation over the now defunct Didcot, Newbury & Southampton line.

By July 1962 Eastleigh was employing 10 Type 3s, mainly on passenger trains, including some of the Waterloo-Bournemouth main line trains, until the heating season necessitated the re-employment of steam locomotives.

In January 1963 Nos D6518/38 went to Worcester for driver training prior to their use on the Fawley-Bromford Bridge oil trains. For a few weeks they could be seen piloting steam engines between Oxford and Hereford.

On 18 November 1963 No D6529 was a last minute substitute for a failed electric locomotive on the 'Royal' special from Gatwick to Victoria for the President of Iceland, while two in multiple were seen on TV departing from Fawley on the first 'Superline' oil tank service to Bromford Bridge, having a train 450 yards long of 54 vehicles grossing some 2,000 tons.

By December 1964 the Eastleigh allocation was 27 — a by-product of the Beeching economies on the SE and Central Divisions!

In 1965, following the decision taken earlier not to electrify from Bournemouth to Weymouth and to adopt push-pull operation, No D6580 was modified for remote operation from electric MU type driving trailers and was tested between Wimbledon Park and Basingstoke with a modified rake of ex-electric MU stock commencing on 21 July 1965. Later, in August 1966, No D6580 ran some high speed tests on the Bournemouth line with newly-delivered 4TC sets. Once the system had been perfected conversion of 19 locomotives was commenced with No D6521 appearing in new guise in September 1966 with drophead, buck-eye couplers and waist-level air pipes and jumpers matching the electric MU stock.

On 10 July 1967 the Bournemouth electrification was inaugurated and Type 3s operated the Weymouth portions of four or eight coaches of TC stock between

Bournemouth and Weymouth, hauling to Weymouth and propelling to Bournemouth.

Blue livery began to be employed from 1967 onwards and the 'D' prefix was dropped from 1968 onwards when the classification became 33. The push-pull version were for a time, in Southern Region records, Class 34 but as this was not authorised by the BR Board they reverted to Class 33 in 1969.

Final classification by BR in January 1974 as follows:

33/0   33.001-65
33/1   33.101-19
33/2   33.201-12

Re-numbering was completed in April 1974 with No 33.008 (D6508).

The Class 33 have also had their accident casualties. The first to be withdrawn was No D6502 in May 1964. On 5 March No D6502 collided at Itchingfield Junction, near Horsham, with a train hauled by No D6565. No D6502 was so badly damaged it was cut-up on the spot. The next casualty was No D6575 which was withdrawn in November 1968 following a collision at Reading. No 33.041 was severely damaged in collision with an eight-car suburban EMU at Bricklayers Arms Junction on 11 September 1975 when a signal aspect was misread. The most recent was No 33.036.

On 11 October 1977, Nos 33.036 and 33.034 hauling a train of 100ton cement tanks struck some wagons of a derailed coal train just west of Mottingham station. No 33.036 ran down the embankment and turned end for end coming to rest on its side in the back garden of a house in Sidcup Road. No 33.043 was recovered the following day, but No 33.036 was finally removed to Hither Green on 26 November and thence to Eastleigh. It was left on the books for some while, being officially withdrawn in July 1979.

In 1980 a decision was made to name four of the class. Nos 33.027 and 33.056 hauled the funeral train of the former Lord Mountbatten of Burma from Waterloo to Romsey and back on 5 September 1979 and they were formally named *Mountbatten of Burma* and *The Burma Star* respectively in September 1980. No 33.008 was named *Eastleigh* on 11 April 1980 and No 22.052 *Ashford* on 17 May 1980. A further locomotive, No 33.025, has since been named *Sultan*.

In later years the class has found a number of duties taking them well away from the Southern Region. Even in their early days pairs were employed on the Cliffe-Uddingstone cement trains as far as York, and the Bromford Bridge oil trains already mentioned. From June 1981 regular workings commenced on the Cardiff-Crewe via Hereford services and from 17 May 1982 they commenced working West Wales Services from Swansea to Fishguard.

Perhaps the $8\frac{1}{2}$ years on the Waterloo-Exeter services were useful in highlighting many of their weaknesses, of which due notice was taken when general overhauls began in 1980. Probably the most useful of all the medium power Bo-Bo types, by virtue of the forward-looking attitude at the time they were specified, they have had a good record of reliability, no doubt aided by the excellent equipment layout and a high degree of standardisation.

Only small departures from the original standard concept exist. Slow speed control was fitted to the Class 33/2s from 1970 onwards for Merry-go-round workings at the new APCM plant at Northfleet and certain colliery/power station duties. 19 locomotives, now classified 33/1 are fitted for push-pull and MU working with electric stock. As new Nos D6565-85 and D6586-97 were delivered without exhaust silencers. Being troublesome, silencers were removed from the whole class. Now environmentalists are pressing for silencers to be re-fitted — such is progress!

9 Keeping Them Running

The principles of preventive maintenance were well covered in the companion book *Class 47 Diesels* and much that was written there applies equally to the Type 2s and 3s. On the other hand the Class 47s were later in the field and so, by-and-large, were handled by depots already having acquired a great deal of experience in maintaining diesel-electric locomotives.

The first Type 2s were pioneers in the field of BR mass-dieselisation and in spite of the fact that it had been intended to set up 'proper maintenance facilities', in many cases the new facilities were either not ready, or only partially completed, and in many cases maintenance was carried out in hastily cleared, partitioned-off sections of existing steam locomotive depots. Much publicity was given to the inauguration of Devons Road depot in East London as the first 'diesel depot' of the modernisation scheme.

Added to lack of proper facilities at first, was the need to train the necessary staff in maintenance depots and main workshops, together with the need for cleanliness, always a problem with steam locomotives either alongside or in the immediate vicinity. Training was carried out with vigour, sometimes assisted by manufacturers' staff ever present in depots and works to advise, and indeed often supervise erection, testing, maintenance procedures and, more important, to attend to 'guarantee' work, modifications, etc.

Class 25 No 25.204 north of Skipton with a Healey Mills-Carlisle coal train, 14 June 1974. *S. Creer*

The first Derby-built Type 2s (later Class 24) after a brief sojourn at Derby, officially allocated to Crewe, in fact went to Hither Green on the Southern Region, a steam depot in the throes of 'conversion' for diesel maintenance, which latter work it performs today. The first BRCW Type 2s (later Class 26) were allocated to Hornsey MPD in North London, where again only 'scratch' facilities existed for their maintenance, since a completely new maintenance depot for the London end of the Great Northern Line was planned, but not completed for some three years or so, at Finsbury Park, Clarence Yard. In any case, at that time steam was a long way from being supplanted, but in spite of that some 50 pilot-scheme locomotives were intended to be maintained in the London area.

But from the start, planned routine preventive maintenance was introduced based on the basis of mandatory examination schedules and to specified standards. This was fine in theory, but at one time Hornsey had to cope with four different locomotive types, none of which had anything in common, and requiring different examination periodicity!

To turn from the general to the specific, over the five classes in this survey there is one basic engine type with relatively minor variations; three different electrical equipment manufacturers, British Thompson-Houston (AEI), Crompton Parkinson/Allen West and GEC (Whitton); two brake equipment manufacturers, Davies & Metcalfe and Westinghouse, one boiler manufacturer, Stones, and two mechanical parts manufacturers, BR and BRCW.

Since commissioning, maintenance schedules have been continuously reviewed and revised, and in general examination and maintenance periods have been extended, since experience has shown that the best results are generally obtained from a really thorough examination carried out at relatively infrequent intervals, rather than a cursory examination made more frequently. This applies particularly to electrical equipment. Also there is little point in removing an engine side cover to look inside a crankcase if all it achieves is to introduce contaminants into the lubricating oil! Safety requirements, of course, have to be met and frequent and thorough examination of bogies, wheels, brake rigging and frames is demanded, together with operational tests on brakes and safety devices.

Regional practices vary, but statutory examination of the above-mentioned parts is done on an average every three days, together with a general interior check for air, oil or coolant leakage, together with a check on the diesel engine lubricating oil and coolant levels. Limiting factors are fuel oil consumption and engine lubricating oil levels, and these largely determine the frequency of 'A' examinations which are carried out at fuelling points and do not necessarily require a visit to a maintenance depot.

Code	Frequency	Work
A	2-4 days	As above
B	250 hours	As A exam plus more comprehensive brake tests. Bogie lubrication check.
C	500 hours	As B, plus electrical machine and control gear inspection. Engine filter change. Bogie clean.
D	2,000 hours	As C, plus fuel injector change and valve tappet adjustment.
E	4,000 hours	As for D, plus other items, eg replacement of traction motor brushes, change cylinder head, etc.

As maintenance is on a time basis some accurate assessment of hours worked is necessary. This is now achieved by the use of TOPS, the Total Operations Processing System, a London-based electronic computer, fed with details of the activities of each locomotive — and, incidentally, the reason for the present classification and numbering system — and declares the status of each locomotive, giving details of when due for examination and the nature thereof.

In recent years locomotives have been concentrated on certain Regions and to relatively few depots on those Regions making the control of maintenance and the rectification of defects easier than hitherto. The remaining Class 25, 26 and 27 are, for example, to be found on the London Midland & Scottish Regions as follows:

Position as at 1 January 1982

Class 25		Class 26		Class 27	
Bescot	27	Haymarket	18	Eastfield	40
Crewe	25	Inverness	33	Inverness	12
Cricklewood	40	*Total*	*51*	Stored	
Eastfield	10			(Serviceable)	4
Haymarket	9			Stored	
Kingsmoor	17			(Unserviceable)	2
Longsight	17			*Total*	*58*
Springs Branch	33				
Toton	24				
Stored					
(Serviceable)	3				
Total	*205*				

Scottish Region locomotives are usually repaired and overhauled either at St Rollox (Glasgow) Works, while they remainder are handled either by Derby or, more recently, Crewe Works.

The Class 33 locomotives are disposed as under:

Eastleigh		Hither Green	
33/0	33	33/0	30
33/1	19	33/2	12
Total	*52*	*Total*	*42*

Scheduled repairs and overhauls are usually carried out by Eastleigh Works, while other repairs are often entrusted to one or other of the Electric Traction Repair Shops, eg Slade Green or Chart Leacon, while for certain work the diesel maintenance depot at West Marina (St Leonard) has been used.

With a common engine design it was only natural that problems common to all five classes would be found, and indeed to be found on the 12-cylinder engines also. Two of these, related to water leakage, have been the source of trouble from time to time on all Sulzer engines, namely deterioration of and leakage from the cylinder block to head water transition bushes. Here a simple rubber bush, encased in a steel tube, has had to be replaced by a more complex rubber/metallic device which now seems to be satisfactory. The other problem area, more so in the early days than today, was the leakage of coolant from the joint between the cylinder liner and block which can only be alleviated by extreme cleanliness and attention to surface finish on assembly.

Mention has been made already of fractures occurring on the earlier 'A' type cylinder heads. While they were all replaced by the later 'B' type on the Class 33 where thermal stressing was high, many 'A' type heads remained in service throughout the lives of the Class 24 and some still remain on Class 26. But having eliminated the cracking problem on the 'A' type heads, a different thermal fatigue problem arose much later on the 'B' type heads, although of a totally different nature. Again the Class 33 were principally affected because of the higher load factors found on Southern Region workings and some cracks were found across the exhaust valve seats. The remedy was firstly to bore out the valve seats to remove the smaller cracks and to fit hard metal valve seat inserts so giving the heads a new lease of life. Those which had cracked too far were replaced by new heads which now have the hard metal inserts fitted from new as standard.

Electrical equipment tends to be complex so that component reliability is important. It has been said, with some truth, that most electrical equipment failures are mechanical! Vibration plays a big part in

Left: **No 25.223 passes Dawlish Warren with the 19.30 Exeter-Paignton, 21 June 1976.** *G. F. Gillham*

Right: **Class 24 Nos 24.073 and 24.057 take the Llandudno line out of Llandudno Junction, 26 June 1977.** *L. Goddard*

Above: **No 26.045 passes Duncraig with the 17.50 Kyle of Lochalsh-Inverness, 8 June 1971.** *G. A. Watt*

Left: **No 27.105 is at the rear of the 16.00 Glasgow-Edinburgh as it leaves Queen Street station, 5 July 1975.** *D. G. Cameron*

Below: **No 33.106 with an Up cement train approaching Battledown flyover.** *A. T. H. Tayler*

traction equipment and 'tractionising' of industrial equipment generally takes the form of designing out the more flimsy parts. This lesson is not always learned easily and considerable experience in diesel traction is often needed before adequate standards of reliability are achieved. Nor is North American experience always a sufficient guide.

With three electrical contractors involved with the locomotives under review, it was natural there would be differences of approach and it is perhaps pertinent to remark that the leanings of British Thompson-Houston/AEI were towards North American design principles, whereas those of Crompton Parkinson were towards European practice, the latter having close connections with the Oerlikon Electrical Company of Switzerland, whereas the former had connections with American General Electric. GEC (Whitton), by comparison, had relatively little diesel traction experience.

Early problems on the British Thompson-Houston equipped Type 2s centred on main generator flashovers and mechanical vibration, leading to fractures of resistances: not big in themselves, but damaging in certain circumstances. The former was largely solved by reducing the shunt field value (increasing the external resistance to reduce the no load voltages) while the vibration-sensitive equipment was made more robust. One big shortcoming, however, was the brushgear on the main generators. Designed to be rotatable so that the bottom brushes could easily be inspected, build up of dirt caused the brush ring to jam and brush inspection was carried out with some reluctance by electricians whose only method of access was to lay on their backs in the oily drip tray. While a modification was made on the later Class 25 generators and was proposed for the Class 24s, it was never implemented. The Class 25s have basically the same main generator, but in their case the brush ring is more easily rotatable, being fitted with a chain mechanism for the purpose. The Crompton main generators on Classes 26 and 33 have a toothed ring which can be rotated easily by fitting a suitable crank on to an external square shaft.

Accessibility is a vital factor which affects maintenance and there is a considerable difference between the equipment layouts of the Class 24/25 and the Class 26/27. On the former all the equipment has to be removed or replaced via the driving cabs, doors, even windows being used, or through small, awkwardly-shaped access panels in the body sides. When some of the Class 25s were fitted with additional air compressors for dual air/vacuum brakes space had to be found, especially difficult on those fitted with train heating boilers, and the position in the gangway severely restricts access, as can be seen from one of the photographs. The other machine, below the brake equipment frame, is the vacuum brake exhauster.

A much cleaner layout is provided by better placing of auxiliary equipment on Classes 26/27, while the absence of a boiler compartment on the Class 33 gives a very clean layout, much appreciated by maintenance staff. The narrow body Class 33/2 are not quite so good, as even the reduction of four inches on gangway width each side of the engine is quite significant.

Class 33 differs fundamentally in its radiator fan drive arrangement. Electric motors drive the radiator fans on all of the Type 2s. These are suspended from the peak of the radiator ducting and constitute a restriction on height at that point. With the increased power equipment of the Class 33, the fan motor would have had to have been bigger and the auxiliary generator capacity greater. It was therefore decided to use a hydrostatic system consisting of one engine-driven pump and a similar hydrostatic fan motor, thermostatically controlled. It has an additional advantage in that a much closer temperature control is possible over the direct engine-driven method, or indeed electric drive.

From the maintenance point of view there are snags. The high line pressures (up to 1,500lb/sq in) in the transmission oil make joint integrity absolutely essential if oil is not to be lost and mess is to be avoided. It took a considerable time to learn how best to deal with the problem, but it now seems to be a satisfactory system, having been adopted in the Class 56 locomotives.

Traction motors are obviously an essential part of the transmission. DC motors still give the best characteristics and at the time the locomotives under review here were conceived there was no alternative. But over the period between 1956 and 1966 considerable development took place. The first BR Type 2s, Class 24 and the first 25 Class 25s had the British Thompson-Houston type 137 motor. Later AEI introduced the 'universal' type 253 motor. Designed for worldwide application and suitable for track gauges of 1 metre and upwards, it is a highly-rated machine for its size and has been used overseas in locomotives of up to 390hp per axle. Here it was required to produce about 240hp per axle. Popular with maintenance staff compared to the larger British Thompson-Houston 137 motors, because the smaller dimensions permitted better accessibility, it has been more sensitive to overheating, resulting either from control gear irregularities or from capacity and in 1975/76 almost 200 traction motors had to be changed at running sheds for inter-pole of field system failures.

The GEC WT 459 motors on the Class 27 locomotives were generally satisfactory until the introduction in 1971 of the Edinburgh-Glasgow push-pull services. The generally high speed level, plus the constant switching of load, led to flashovers, mainly from brush gear support weakness, and armature banding failures. Even suspension bearings worked loose in their housings and gearwheels suffered undue wear and it was almost a maintenance man's nightmare to keep services running until the problems were overcome. Mechanical parts suffered too and even the traction motor nose suspensions had to be modified to eliminate vibration.

Classes 26 and 33 employ the Crompton Parkinson C.171 traction motor. There are three variants, two in Class 26 and the third covers all of the Class 33s. One major panic resulted in a hasty check of all armature shafts following breakages on similar machines on Class 45s in 1963. Shafts were checked by ultrasonics and those found suspect were subsequently changed.

A major enemy of electrical machines is cast iron laden oily dirt and quite elaborate steps have to be taken to keep such out of traction motors. Where forced-ventilation is employed, as in all of the locomotives covered by this book, steps have to be taken to ensure that the means of conveying clean air from the body-mounted traction motor blowers to the motors does not permit the entry of oil to brush gear or commutators — another problem since flexible bellows or something similar have to be provided between underframe and motors, and these are subject to wear and tear.

Quite apart from track induced vibration, any diesel engine has certain vibration characteristics and for that reason engines are often, as in this case, mounted on rubber pads, or even sophisticated special mountings. It was with some surprise, early in 1961, when running with a freight train at about $\frac{2}{3}$ power, the driver of a Class 33 saw his controller handle drop off. The main shaft carrying the rather heavy handle had fractured and the metal had fatigued due to being subjected to a fairly high frequency vibration. The train was not a complete failure because, fortunately, the duplicate off-side handle was still intact! Shafts were quickly increased in size and the problem did not recur. In the Class 33 it was found that the natural frequency of the frame corresponded to the 4th order frequency of the engine when running at about 660rpm. No significant improvement could be made by changing engine mounting pads because there was insufficient room to instal mountings of the type needed. Subsequently, to alleviate other vibration-prone problems, quite small changes were made to fastenings and mounting details.

These are but a few of the items which may arise in the cause of keeping locomotives on the road. To cover the whole subject adequately would require a book of its own. Perhaps one day somebody will find the time to give a layman's account of diesel locomotive running and maintenance.

Above left: **No 33.005 climbs out of Buckhorn Weston tunnel with the 11.00 Exeter-Waterloo, 27 May 1978.** *G. F. Gillham*

Left: **The 14.10 Waterloo-Salisbury train approaches Oakley behind No 33.019.** *A. T. H. Tayler*

Right: **Class 26 No 5337 calling at Dingwall with the 08.15 Kyle-Inverness train, 11 October 1973.** *P. J. Fowler*

10 Epilogue

This chapter briefly summarises what has gone before. The BR Type 2 was selected to be the 'standard' Type 2 and Classes 24 and 25 totalled 478 locomotives. There were variants, some 13 in all, some of them very minor, as can generally be found with any large run as improvements are introduced. They were built between 1958 and 1967. The Class 24s have all gone, although one remains privately preserved and three are 'service' vehicles, one used as a locomotive from time to time; the other two being used as generators.

Of the 327 examples of Class 25, 205 remained on 1 January 1982. At the time of writing, politics, nationally and internally, seem to indicate they too will have a relatively short life. Never so reliable as their contractor-built counter-parts or so easy to repair or maintain, it is doubtful if many will achieve their 'Book Life' of 20 years.

Medium power, mixed traffic locomotives are never very spectacular, but perhaps the more popular locomotives were the 47 Class 26 and 69 Class 27s built by the former Birmingham Railway Carriage & Wagon Company of Smethwick. Today 41 Class 26 survive and may be found in most parts of the Scottish Region north of Edinburgh and Glasgow. Plans are in hand to refurbish the majority over the next five years in spite of drafting in Class 37s, sufficient proof of their usefulness and inherent reliability.

Of the 69 Class 27s only 56 remained on the books at 1 January 1982, and of those two were stored unserviceable. Now the Edinburgh-Glasgow services are covered by the Class 47/7s, the Class 27/1 and 27/2 variants and having a somewhat easier life — indeed two of the Class 27/2s have been withdrawn from service. While it is intended to refurbish some, it is not likely to exceed half of the number now in

Above: **No 27.037 arrives at Taynuilt with the 12.55 Glasgow-Oban, 22 March 1978.** *J. Sagar*

Left: **No 25.283 approaches Gresty No 1 signalbox with a Crewe-Cardiff service, 26 May 1978.** *B. J. Nicolle*

Above right: **Class 25 No 25.224 at Coombe Junction on the Looe branch, 14 September 1976.** *G. F. Roose*

Right: **No 24.082 at Northgate Locks, Chester on 23 May 1978.** *L. Goddard*

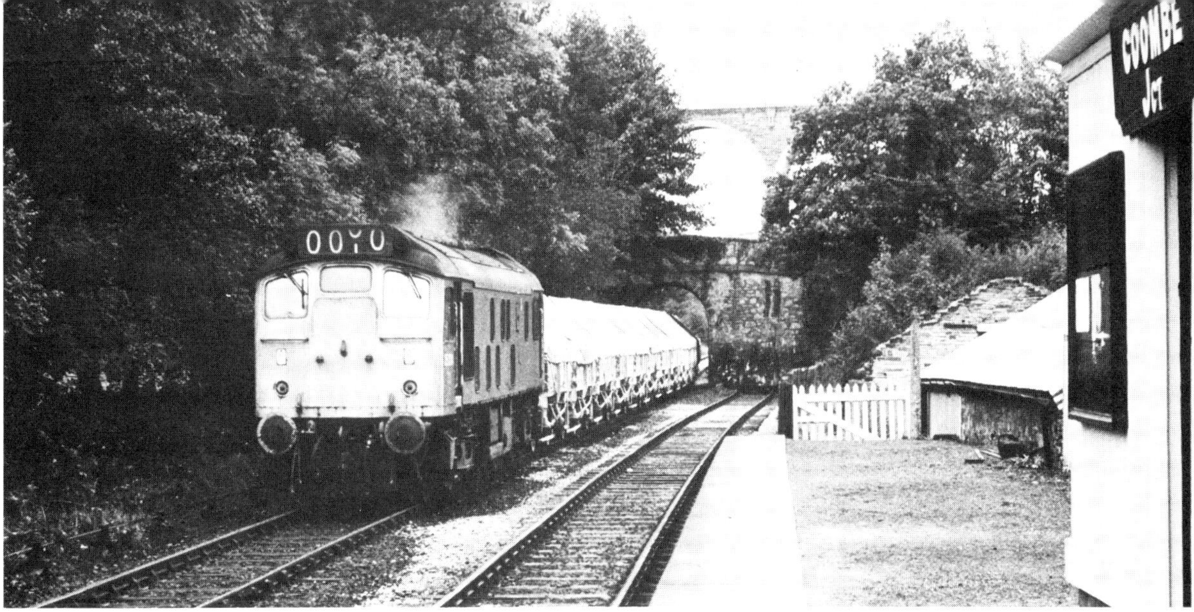
COOMBE
Jct

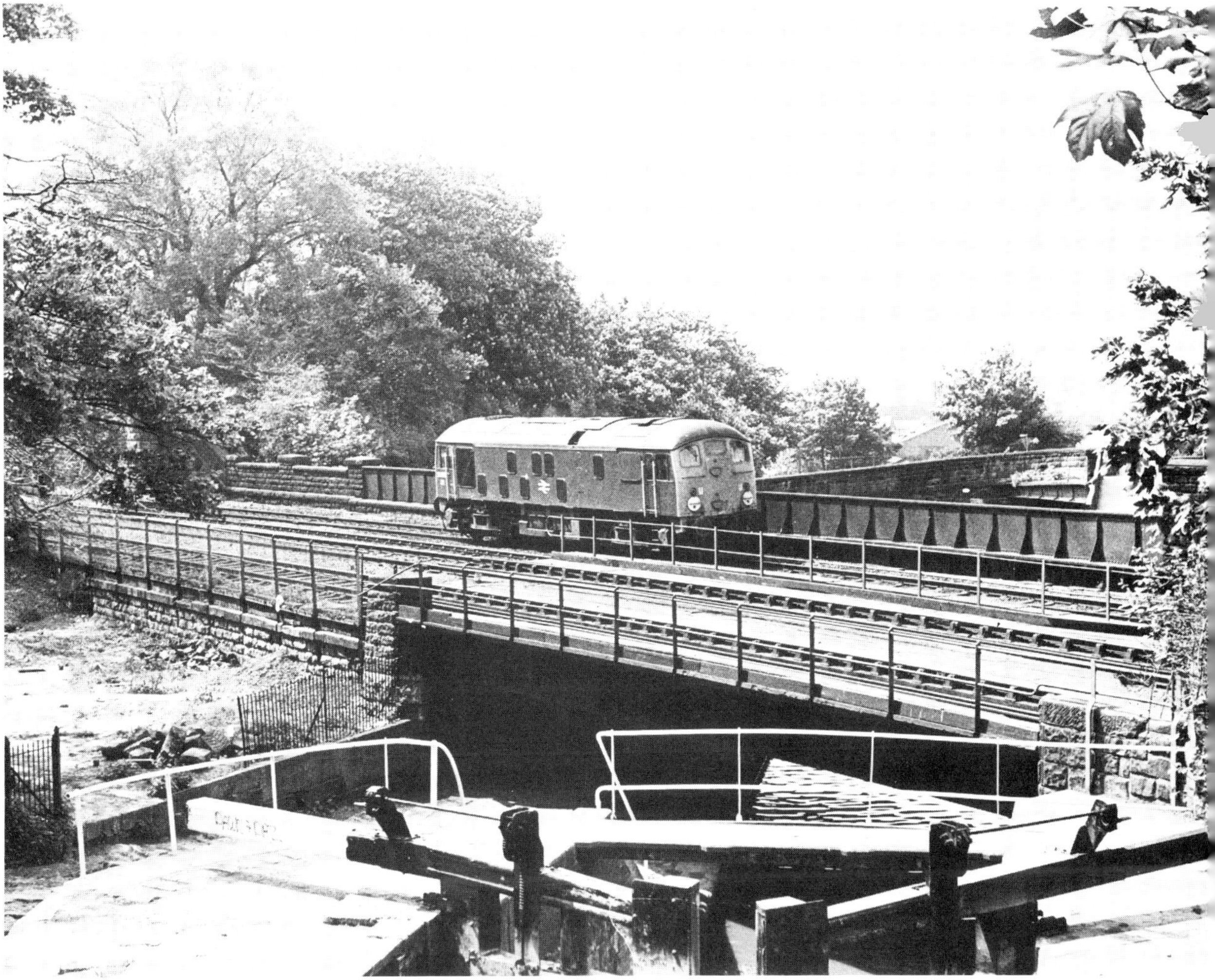

service; that is assuming the Scottish Region remains the size it is today and the lines from Inverness to the North and the Kyle of Lochalsh with Fort William to Mallaig remain.

It is interesting to reflect on the hasty modifications carried out on the 24 Class 27s for the Edinburgh-Glasgow push-pull service. Not push-pull in the usual sense of the term since trains were operated with a locomotive at each end, more a multiple unit operation with locomotives in place of power cars. It is not generally known that it was intended to employ a small gas turbine to provide power for electric train heating and some considerable time was spent in trying to adapt a unit, already in operation in aircraft de-icing and auxiliary generator plants.

A small compact gas turbine, developed by David Budworth Ltd of Harwich was intended to be coupled through a 12.5:1 reduction gearbox to a Houchin 120kW alternator, the gearbox being a two-stage epi-cyclic box, part of the gas turbine. Locomotive No D5391 (later 27.119 and 27.201) was fitted up for an acceptance test on the prototype gas turbine alternator set. A 50-hour test schedule was run at the manufacturer's works at 90kW satisfactorily, subject to the engine being subsequently rated at 130kW. For a number of reasons the project failed, one important reason being the inability of the turbine to reach its expected output and efficiency. The first batch of locomotives to be modified by Derby Works retained their Stones Vapour Steam generators and had to enter service heating the trains by steam. The company eventually went into liquidation following the tragic death in an air accident of Mr David Budworth.

The second 12 locomotives were later equipped with 120kW diesel alternator sets. A Deutz air-cooled type F8L413, 8-cylinder engine coupled to a Houchin 120kW alternator was mounted in the boiler compartment of 12 locomotives which were re-classified 27/2.

The Class 33 locomotives, built by the Birmingham Railway Carriage & Wagon Company of Smethwick, numbered 86 of standard width and a further 12 of reduced profile to enable them to work between Tonbridge and Battle on the Hastings line — 98 locomotives in all. At 1 January 1982 a total of 94 were in service with one 33.056 in doubt as to its future following serious damage sustained in a collision at Earlsfield on 10 October 1981.

Class 33 is one of the classes earmarked for 'life' extension into the 1990s and general overhauls at Eastleigh are already taking this into account. Originally considered oddities by other Regions on account of their air brakes and electric train heating, they have proved their worth not only on the Southern Region, where they are 'maids of all work', but have been coveted in more recent times by other Regions. Not so long ago the Scottish Region were trying to get 30 of them, but this was successfully resisted!

Now, as already noted, their utilisation is being widened to cover the Cardiff-Crewe and Cardiff-Swansea-West Wales services, still being maintained on the Southern Region. Not without their problems they still, nevertheless, give excellent service and must certainly have amply justified the stand made by the Region against the BTC in 1958.

With changing traffic patterns and the passage of time these 692 locomotives employing one basic make of engine have now been whittled down to 398 on BR's books. The outstanding performers have been the Class 26s and 33s, perhaps going some way towards vindicating the criticism levelled at the private locomotive builders and contractors in another recent book. Through them the BRCW is remembered, although it went out of business after the last Class 27 was delivered.

Never very glamorous, the medium-power locomotives nevertheless have their followers. Today, their utilisation patterns are changing and many have important main line tasks to perform, albeit often in pairs. It is still encouraging that many have an important role to fulfil for a number of years to come. It is hoped this account has given a clear picture of the life and work of the Sulzer-engined Bo-Bo diesel-electric locomotives of British Railways.

Left: **A Waterloo-Exeter train passing Farnborough behind No 33.012, September 1979.** *A. T. H. Tayler*

Top: **Nos 33.013 and 33.112 dropping down towards Westbury with stone hoppers near Upton Scudamore, 21 July 1978.** *M. Mitchell*

Above: **No 33.025 Sultan with the 15.10 Crawford Central-Crewe on 20 March 1982.** *John S. Whiteley*

Right: **No 33.018 heads the 12.00 Swansea-Fishguard Harbour train on the start of the climb to Cockett Summit on 12 February 1983.** *S. K. Miles*

Appendix: Class Data

Class 24

Orig No	TOPS No	To Stock	Withdrawn	Diagram	Weight (T)	Boiler	Builder	Notes
5000	24.005	8/58 5B SR	10/75 65A	24-a/V	79.8	Yes	Derby	Marylebone 24/7/58
5001	24.001	10/58 5B SR	10/75 D.05	24-a/V	79.8	Yes	Derby	
5002	24.002	11/58 5B SR	10/75	24-a/V	79.8	Yes	Derby	
5003	24.003	11/58 5B SR	8/75	24-a/V	79.8	Yes	Derby	
5004	24.004	12/58 5B SR	10/75	24-a/V	79.8	Yes	Derby	
5005	—	12/58 5B SR	1/69 D.05	24-a/V	79.8	Yes	Derby	
5006	24.006	1/59 5B SR	8/75	24-a/V	79.8	Yes	Derby	
5007	24.007	2/59 5B SR	10/75	24-a/V	79.8	Yes	Derby	
5008	24.008	2/59 73C SR	8/75	24-a/V	79.8	Yes	Derby	
5009	24.009	3/59 73C SR D.05	7/76 HA	24-a/V	79.8	Yes	Derby	
5010	24.010	3/59 73C SR	10/75 D.05	24-a/V	79.8	Yes	Derby	
5011	24.011	3/59 73C SR	10/75	24-a/V	79.8	Yes	Derby	
5012	24.012	4/59 73C SR	8/75	24-a/V	79.8	Yes	Derby	
5013	24.013	4/59 73C SR	10/75	24-a/V	79.8	Yes	Derby	
5014	24.014	4/59 73C SR	10/75	24-a/V	79.8	Yes	Derby	
5015	24.015	5/59 5B	8/75	24-a/V	79.8	Yes	Derby	
5016	24.016	5/59 5B	8/75	24-a/V	79.8	Yes	Derby	
5017	24.017	5/59 73C SR	10/75	24-a/V	79.8	Yes	Derby	
5018	24.018	6/59 5B	8/75	24-a/V	79.8	Yes	Derby	
5019	24.019	7/59 5B	10/75	24-a/V	79.8	Yes	Derby	
5020	24.020	8/59 17A	8/75	24-b/V	78.7	Yes	Derby	
5021	24.021	8/59 32B	8/75	24-b/V	78.7	Yes	Derby	
5022	24.022	9/59 32B	1/76	24-b/V	78.7	Yes	Derby	
5023	24.023	9/59 32B	9/78 CD	24-b/V	78.7	Yes	Derby	
5024	24.024	10/59 32B	8/75	24-b/V	78.7	Yes	Derby	
5025	24.025	10/59 32B	1/76	24-b/V	78.7	Yes	Derby	
5026	24.026	10/59 32B	8/75	24-b/V	78.7	Yes	Derby	
5027	24.027	10/59 32B	7/76 CD	24-b/V	78.7	Yes	Derby	
5028	24.028	11/59 32B	6/72 D.05	24-b/V	78.7	Yes	Derby	
5029	24.029	11/59 32B	8/75	24-b/V	78.7	Yes	Derby	
5030	24.030	6/59 31B	7/76	24-b/V	78.7	Yes	Crewe	
5031	24.031	6/59 31B	10/75	24-b/V	78.7	Yes	Crewe	
5032	24.032	7/59 31B	7/76	24-b/V	78.7	Yes	Crewe	Preserved N York Moors
5033	24.033	8/59 31B	10/75	24-b/V	78.7	Yes	Crewe	
5034	24.034	9/59 31B	1/76	24-b/V	78.7	Yes	Crewe	
5035	24.035	8/59 31B	10/78 CD	24-b/V	78.7	Yes	Crewe	
5036	24.036	9/59 31B	11/77 CD	24-b/V	78.7	Yes	Crewe	
5037	24.037	9/59 31B	7/76 CD	24-b/V	78.7	Yes	Crewe	
5038	24.038	9/59 32B	7/76 CD	24-b/V	78.7	Yes	Crewe	
5039	24.039	9/59 32B	7/76 CD	24-b/V	78.7	Yes	Crewe	
5040	24.040	10/59 32B	1/76	24-b/V	78.7	Yes	Crewe	
5041	24.041	9/59 32B	8/75 CD	24-b/V	78.7	Yes	Crewe	
5042	24.042	10/59 32B	8/75	24-b/V	78.7	Yes	Crewe	
5043		10/59 32B	8/69 D.05	24-b/V	78.7	Yes	Crewe	

Orig No	TOPS No	To Stock	Withdrawn	Diagram	Weight (T)	Boiler	Builder	Notes
5044	24.044	10/59 32B	1/76	24-c/V	77.0	Yes	Crewe	
5045	24.045	11/59 31B	8/75	24-c/V	77.0	Yes	Crewe	
5046	24.046	11/59 31B	7/76 CD	24-c/V	77.0	Yes	Crewe	
5047	24.047	11/59 31B	11/78 CD	24-c/V	77.0	Yes	Crewe	
5048	24.048	11/59 31B	8/75	24-c/V	77.0	Yes	Crewe	
5049	24.049	4/60 31B	1/76	24-c/V	77.0	Yes	Crewe	
5050	24.050	11/59 31B	10/75	24-1a/V	73.0	Yes	Crewe	
5051		12/59 31B	11/67 65A	24-1a/V	73.0	Yes	Crewe	
5052	24.052	12/59 31B	12/76 CD	24-1a/V	73.0	Yes	Crewe	
5053	24.053	12/59 31B	1/76	24-1a/V	73.0	Yes	Crewe	
5054	24.054	12/59 31B	7/76 CD	24-1a/V	73.0	Yes	Crewe	TED968008 Preserved, Bury
5055	24.055	12/59 31B	10/75	24-1a/V	73.0	Yes	Crewe	
5056	24.056	12/59 31B	10/75	24-1a/V	73.0	Yes	Crewe	
5057	24.057	12/59 31B	1/78 CD	24-1a/V	73.0	Yes	Crewe	
5058	24.058	1/60 31B	10/75	24-1a/V	73.0	Yes	Crewe	
5059	24.059	12/59 31B	10/75	24-1a/V	73.0	Yes	Crewe	
5060	24.060	1-60 31B	10/75	24-1a/V	73.0	Yes	Crewe	
5061	24.061	1/60 31B	8/75	24-1a/V	73.0	Yes	Crewe	97201 968007
5062	24.062	1/60 31B	10/75	24-1a/V	73.0	Yes	Crewe	
5063	24.063	1/60 31B	4/79 CD	24-1a/V	73.0	Yes	Crewe	
5064	24.064	1/60 31B	1/76	24-1a/V	73.0	Yes	Crewe	
5065	24.065	2/60 31B	12/76	24-1a/V	73.0	Yes	Crewe	
5066	24.066	12/59 31B	2/76	24-1a/V	73.0	Yes	Derby	
5067		12/59 31B	10/76 64B	24-1a/V	73.0	Yes	Derby	
5068		12/59 34G	10/72 64B	24-1a/V	73.0	Yes	Derby	1st Blue Dec '66
5069	24.069	1/60 31B	12/76 HA	24-1a/V	73.0	Yes	Derby	
5070	24.070	1/60 31B	2/76	24-1a/V	73.0	Yes	Derby	
5071	24.071	2/60 31B	8/75	24-1a/V	73.0	Yes	Derby	
5072	24.072	2/60 31B	10/75	24-1a/V	73.0	Yes	Derby	
5073	24.073	3/60 31B	2/76	24-1a/V	73.0	Yes	Derby	
5074	24.074	3/60 IC	10/75	24-1a/V	73.0	Yes	Derby	
5075	24.075	3/60 31B	1/76	24-1a/V	73.0	Yes	Derby	
5076	24.076	2/60 31B	10/75	24-1a/V	73.0	Yes	Crewe	
5077	24.077	2/60 31B	7/76 CD	24-1a/V	73.0	Yes	Crewe	
5078	24.078	2/60 31B	4/76	24-1a/V	73.0	Yes	Crewe	
5079	24.079	2/60 2A	7/76 CD	24-1a/V	73.0	Yes	Crewe	
5080	24.080	3/60 1A	9/76 CD	24-1a/V	73.0	Yes	Crewe	
5081	24.081	3/60 2A	10/80 CD	24-1a/V	73.0	Yes	Crewe	Last of class, Preserved, Southport
5082	24.082	3/60 31B	3/79 CD	24-1a/V	73.0	Yes	Crewe	
5083	24.083	4/60 31B	3/76	24-1a/V	73.0	Yes	Crewe	
5084	24.084	4/60 2A	7/76 CD	24-1a/V	73.0	Yes	Crewe	
5085	24.085	8/60 31B	7/76 CD	24-1a/V	73.0	Yes	Crewe	
5086	24.086	5/60 31B	1/76	24-1a/V	73.0	Yes	Crewe	
5087	24.087	6/60 31B	2/78 CD	24-1a/V	73.0	Yes	Crewe	
5088		6/60 31B	7/70 D.05	24-1a/V	73.0	Yes	Crewe	
5089	24.089	6/60 14A	1/76	24-1a/V	73.0	Yes	Crewe	
5090	24.090	6/60 31B	2/76	24-1a/V	73.0	Yes	Crewe	
5091	24.091	6/60 41A	11/77 CD	24-1a/V	73.0	Yes	Crewe	
5092	24.092	7/60 14A	10/75	24-1a/V	73.0	Yes	Crewe	
5093		7/60 1A	8/65 D.05	24-1a/V	73.0	Yes	Crewe	
5094	24.094	2/60 30A	12/76	24-1a/V	73.0	Yes	Darlington	
5095	24.095	3/60 34G	8/75	24-1a/V	73.0	Yes	Darlington	
5096	24.096	3/60 52A	8/75	24-1a/V	73.0	Yes	Darlington	
5097	24.097	5/60 52A	2/76	24-1a/V	73.0	Yes	Darlington	
5098	24.098	5/60 52A	8/75	24-1a/V	73.0	Yes	Darlington	
5099	24.099	6/60 52A	2/76	24-1a/V	73.0	Yes	Darlington	
5100	24.100	6/60 52A	2/76	24-1a/V	73.0	Yes	Darlington	
5101	24.101	7/60 52A	2/76	24-1a/V	73.0	Yes	Darlington	
5102	24.102	7/60 52A	2/76	24-1b/V	71.0	No	Darlington	
5103	24.103	8/60 52A	12/76	24-1b/V	71.0	No	Darlington	
5104	24.104	8/60 52A	12/76	24-1b/V	71.0	No	Darlington	
5105	24.105	9/60 52A	10/75	24-1b/V	71.0	No	Darlington	
5106	24.106	9/60 52A	12/76	24-1b/V	71.0	No	Darlington	
5107	24.107	10/60 52A	12/76	24-1b/V	71.0	No	Darlington	
5108	24.108	10/60 52A	7/76	24-1b/V	71.0	No	Darlington	
5109	24.109	11/60 52A	2/76	24-1b/V	71.0	No	Darlington	
5110	24.110	11/60 52A	12/76	24-1b/V	71.0	No	Darlington	
5111	24.111	11/60 52A	2/76	24-1b/V	71.0	No	Darlington	
5112	24.112	12/60 52A	12/76	24-1a/V	73.0	Yes	Darlington	

Orig No	TOPS No	To Stock	Withdrawn		Weight (T)	Boiler	Builder	Notes
5113	24.113	1/61 52A	12/76	24-1a/V	73.0	Yes	Darlington	
5114		4/60 60A	10/73 60A	24-1a/V	73.0	Yes	Derby	
5115	24.115	5/60 60A	12/76	24-1a/V	73.0	Yes	Derby	
5116	24.116	5/60 60A	9/76 HA	24-1a/V	73.0	Yes	Derby	
5117	24.117	5/60 60A	2/76	24-1a/V	73.0	Yes	Derby	
5118	24.118	5/60 60A	12/76	24-1a/V	73.0	Yes	Derby	
5119	24.119	6/60 60A		24-1a/V	73.0	Yes	Derby	
5120	24.120	6/60 60A	12/76	24-1a/V	73.0	Yes	Derby	
5121	24.121	6/60 60A	12/76	24-1a/V	73.0	Yes	Derby	
5122		6/60 60A	9/68 60A	24-1a/V	73.0	Yes	Derby	
5123	24.123	6/60 60A	7/76 HA	24-1a/V	73.0	Yes	Derby	
5124	24.124	7/60 60A	12/76	24-1a/V	73.0	Yes	Derby	
5125	24.125	7/60 60A	3/76	24-1a/V	73.0	Yes	Derby	
5126	24.126	7/60 60A	2/76	24-1a/V	73.0	Yes	Derby	
5127	24.127	7/60 60A	2/76	24-1a/V	73.0	Yes	Derby	
5128	24.128	8/60 60A	7/76	24-1a/V	73.0	Yes	Derby	
5129	24.129	8/60 60A	12/76	24-1a/V	73.0	Yes	Derby	
5130	24.130	9/60 60A	12/76	24-1a/V	73.0	Yes	Derby	
5131		9/60 60A	9/71 60A	24-1a/V	73.0	Yes	Derby	
5132	24.132	9/60 60A	2/76	24-1a/V	73.0	Yes	Derby	
5133	24.133	9/60 9A	3/78 CD	24-1a/V	73.0	Yes	Derby	
5134	24.134	9/60 9A	12/76	24-1a/V	73.0	Yes	Derby	
5135	24.135	9/60 9A	1/76	24-1a/V	73.0	Yes	Derby	
5136	24.136	10/60 9A	10/75	24-1a/V	73.0	Yes	Derby	
5137	24.137	10/60 9A	7/76	24-1a/V	73.0	Yes	Derby	
5138		10/60 9A	8/69 D.05	24-1a/V	73.0	Yes	Derby	
5139		10/60 9A	8/69 D.05	24-1a/V	73.0	Yes	Derby	
5140	24.140	11/60 9A	1/76	24-1a/V	73.0	Yes	Derby	
5141	24.141	11/60 9A	7/76 CD	24-1a/V	73.0	Yes	Derby	
5142	24.142	11/60 9A	7/76 CD	24-1a/V	73.0	Yes	Derby	TBD968009
5143	24.143	11/60 1A	1/76	24-1a/V	73.0	Yes	Derby	
5144	24.144	11/60 1A	1/76	24-1a/V	73.0	Yes	Derby	
5145	24.145	12/60 1A	1/76	24-1a/V	73.0	Yes	Derby	
5146	24.146	12/60 1A	1/76	24-1a/V	73.0	Yes	Derby	
5147	24.147	12/60 52A	7/76 HA	24-1a/V	73.0	Yes	Derby	
5148	24.148	12/60 52A	10/75	24-1a/V	73.0	Yes	Derby	
5149		2/61 52A	10/73 65A	24-1a/V	73.0	Yes	Derby	
5150	24.150	2/61 52A	12/76	24-1a/V	73.0	Yes	Derby	

Class 25

Orig No	TOPS No	To Stock	Withdrawn	Diagram	Weight (T)	Boiler	Tr Motor Type	Builder
5151	25.001	4/61 51L	9/80 ED	25-1a/V	70.25	No	137BX	Darlington
5152	25.002	5/61 51L	12/80ED	25-1a/V	70.25	No	137BX	Darlington
5153	25.003	5/61 51L	8/76 ED	25-1a/V	70.25	No	137BX	Darlington
5154	25.004	5/61 51L	9/76 ED	25-1a/V	70.25	No	137BX	Darlington
5155	25.005	6/61 51L	12/80 ED	25-1a/V	70.25	No	137BX	Darlington
5156	25.006	6/61 51L	11/80 ZL	25-1a/V	70.25	No	137BX	Darlington
5157	25.007	7/61 51L	12/80 ZL	25-1a/V	70.25	No	137BX	Darlington
5158	25.008	7/61 51L	6/80 HA	25-1a/V	70.25	No	137BX	Darlington
5159	25.009	7/61 51L	7/80 HA	25-1a/V	70.25	No	137BX	Darlington
5160	25.010	8/61 51L	12/80 HA	25-1a/V	70.25	No	137BX	Darlington
5161	25.011	9/61 51L	12/80 HA	25-1a/V	70.25	No	137BX	Darlington
5162	25.012	9/61 51L	2/77 HA	25-1a/V	70.25	No	137BX	Darlington
5163	25.013	9/61 51L	9/80 HA	25-1a/V	70.25	No	137BX	Darlington
5164	25.014	10/61 51L	7/77 ED	25-1a/V	70.25	No	137BX	Darlington
5165	25.015	10/61 51L	12/75 TI	25-1a/V	70.25	No	137BX	Darlington
5166	25.016	11/61 51L	1/76 TI	25-b/V	72.35	No	137BX	Darlington
5167	25.017	11/61 51L	1/76 TI	25-b/V	72.35	No	137BX	Darlington
5168	25.018	12/61 51L	11/76 ED	25-b/V	72.35	No	137BX	Darlington
5169	25.019	12/61 51L	9/80 HA	25-b/V	72.35	No	137BX	Darlington
5170	25.020	12/61 51L	1/76 TI	25-b/V	72.35	No	137BX	Darlington
5171	25.021	2/62 51L	9/80 HA	25-b/V	72.35	No	137BX	Darlington
5172	25.022	2/62 51L	1/76 TI	25-b/V	72.35	No	137BX	Darlington
5173	25.023	3/62 51L	9/80 HA	25-b/V	73.35	No	137BX	Darlington
5174	25.024	3/62 51L	1/76 TI	25-b/V	72.35	No	137BX	Darlington
5175	25.025	4/62 51L	4/77 ED	25-b/V	72.35	No	137BX	Darlington
5176	25.026	1/63 55A	11/80 TO	25-1a/V	73.75	Yes	253AY	Darlington
5177	25.027	2/63 55A		25-1a/V	73.75	Yes	253AY	Darlington
5178	25.028	2/63 55A	12/80 HA	25-2c/X	74.8	Yes	253AY	Darlington
5179	25.029	2/63 52A	8/77 TO	25-1b/V	71.45	No	253AY	Darlington
5180	25.030	2/63 52A	8/76 CW	25-1b/V	71.45	No	253AY	Darlington

Orig No	TOPS No	To Stock	Withdrawn	Diagram	Weight (T)	Boiler	Tr Motor Type	Builder
5181	25.031	3/63 52A	12/77 ED	25-1b/V	71.45	No	253AY	Darlington
5182	25.032	3/63 52A		25-1b/X	71.45	No	253AY	Darlington
5183	25.033	4/63 18A		25-2c/X	74.4	Yes	253AY	Darlington
5184	25.034	5/63 18A		25-2c/X	74.4	Yes	253AY	Darlington
5185	25.035	5/63 18A		25-2c/X	74.4	Yes	253AY	Darlington
5186	25.036	3/63 18A		25-2c/X	74.4	Yes	253AY	Derby
5187	25.037	3/63 18A		25-2c/X	74.4	Yes	253AY	Derby
5188	25.038	3/63 18A	5/81 KD	25-1a/V	73.75	Yes	253AY	Derby
5189	25.039	4/63 18A	5/81 LO	25-1a/V	73.75	Yes	253AY	Derby
5190	25.040	4/63 18A	11/80 LO	25-1a/V	73.75	Yes	253AY	Derby
5191	25.041	4/63 18A	5/81 KD	25-1a/V	73.75	Yes	253AY	Derby
5192	25.042	5/63 18A		25-1a/V	73.75	Yes	253AY	Derby
5193	25.043	5/63 18A	2/81 CD	25-1a/V	73.75	Yes	253AY	Derby
5194	25.044	5/63 18A		25-2c/X	73.75	Yes	253AY	Derby
5195	25.045	5/63 18A	10/75 HA	25-2c/X	73.75	Yes	253AY	Derby
5196	25.046	5/63 18A	2/81 HA	25-2c/X	73.75	Yes	253AY	Derby
5197	25.047	6/63 18A	9/80 SP	25-2c/X	73.75	Yes	253AY	Derby
5198	25.048	6/63 18A		25-2c/X	73.75	Yes	253AY	Derby
5199	25.049	6/63 18A		25-2c/X	73.75	Yes	253AY	Derby
5200	25.050	6/63 18A		25-2c/X	74.4	Yes	253AY	Derby
5201	25.051	6/63 18A		25-2c/X	74.4	Yes	253AY	Derby
5202	25.052	6/63 18A	10/80 LA	25-2c/X	74.4	Yes	253AY	Derby
5203	25.053	6/63 18A	12/80 BS/ZL	25-2c/X	74.4	Yes	253AY	Derby
5204	25.054	6/63 18A		25-2c/X	74.4	Yes	253AY	Derby
5205	25.055	6/63 18A	11/80 KD	25-2c/X	74.4	Yes	253AY	Derby
5206	25.056	6/63 18A		25-2c/X	74.4	Yes	253AY	Derby
5207	25.057	7/63 18A		25-2c/X	74.4	Yes	253AY	Derby
5208	25.058	7/63 18A		25-2c/X	74.4	Yes	253AY	Derby
5209	25.059	7/63 18A		25-2c/X	74.4	Yes	253AY	Derby
5210	25.060	7/63 18A		25-2c/X	74.4	Yes	253AY	Derby
5211	25.061	7/63 18A	11/80 LO	25-2c/X	74.4	Yes	253AY	Derby
5212	25.062	7/63 18A		25-2c/X	74.4	Yes	253AY	Derby
5213	25.063	7/63 18A	11/80 CD	25-2c/X	74.4	Yes	253AY	Derby
5214	25.064	7/63 18A		25-2c/X	74.4	Yes	253AY	Derby
5215	25.065	7/63 18A	2/81 HA	25-2c/X	74.4	Yes	253AY	Derby
5216	25.066	7/63 18A	6/81 CW	25-2c/X	74.4	Yes	253AY	Derby
5217	25.067	8/63 18A		25-2c/X	74.4	Yes	253AY	Derby
5218	25.068	8/63 14A	7/80 ED	25-2c/X	74.4	Yes	253AY	Derby
5219	25.069	8/63 18A		25-2c/X	74.4	Yes	253AY	Derby
5220	25.070	9/63 14A	11/80 SP	25-2c/X	74.4	Yes	253AY	Derby
5221	25.071	8/63 14A	6/81 LO	25-2c/X	74.4	Yes	253AY	Derby
5222	25.072	9/63 14A		25-2c/X	74.4	Yes	253AY	Derby
5223	25.073	7/63 18A	9/81 TO	25-2c/X	74.4	Yes	253AY	Darlington
5224	25.074	7/63 18A	9/81 TO	25-2c/X	74.4	Yes	253AY	Darlington
5225	25.075	7/63 18A	9	25-2c/X	74.4	Yes	253AY	Darlington
5226	25.076	8/63 18A		25-2c/X	74.4	Yes	253AY	Darlington
5227	25.077	8/63 18A	8/78 ED	25-2c/X	74.4	Yes	253AY	Darlington
5228	25.078	9/63 14A		25-2c/X	74.4	Yes	253AY	Darlington
5229	25.079	9/63 14A		25-2c/X	74.4	Yes	253AY	Darlington
5230	25.080	10/63 14A		25-2c/X	74.4	Yes	253AY	Darlington
5231	25.081	12/63 16A	2/82 CW	25-2c/X	74.4	Yes	253AY	Darlington
5232	25.082	11/63 16A	5/81 HA	25-2c/X	74.4	Yes	253AY	Darlington
5233	25.083	12/63 16A		25-2a/V	73.05	Yes	253AY	Derby
5234	25.084	12/63 16A		25-2a/V	73.05	Yes	253AY	Derby
5235	25.085	12/63 16A	3/82 KD	25-2a/V	73.05	Yes	253AY	Derby
5236	25.086	12/63 16A		25-2a/V	73.05	Yes	253AY	Derby
5237	25.087	12/63 16A	9/80 HA	25-2a/V	73.05	Yes	253AY	Derby
5238	25.088	12/63 16A	8/81 LO	25-2b/X	70.7	No	253AY	Derby
5239	25.089	1/64 16A		25-2b/X	70.7	No	253AY	Derby
5240	25.090	1/64 16A		25-2b/X	70.7	No	253AY	Derby
5241	25.091	1/64 16A	10/78 HA	25-2b/X	70.7	No	253AY	Derby
5242	25.092	1/64 16A	5/80 CW	25-2b/X	70.7	No	253AY	Derby
5243	25.093	1/64 16A		25-2b/X	70.7	No	253AY	Derby
5244	25.094	1/64 16A	2/81 TO	25-2b/X	70.7	No	253AY	Derby
5245	25.095	1/64 16A		25-2b/X	70.7	No	253AY	Derby
5246	25.096	2/64 16A	12/77 ED	25-2b/X	70.7	No	253AY	Derby
5247	25.097	2/64 16A		25-2b/X	70.7	No	253AY	Derby
5248	25.098	2/64 16A	10/78 ED	25-2b/X	70.7	No	253AY	Derby
5249	25.099	2/64 16A	12/80 CW/ZL	25-2b/X	70.7	No	253AY	Derby
5250	25.100	2/64 16A	2/81 LO	25-2b/X	70.7	No	253AY	Derby
5251	25.101	3/64 16A		25-2b/X	70.7	No	253AY	Derby
5252	25.102	3/64 16A	5/80 LO	25-2b/X	70.7	No	253AY	Derby
5253	25.103	3/64 16A	9/80 SP	25-2b/X	70.7	No	253AY	Derby

Orig No	TOPS No	To Stock	Withdrawn	Diagram	Weight (T)	Boiler	Tr Motor Type	Builder
5254	25.104	3/64 16A		25-2b/X	70.7	No	253AY	Derby
5255	25.105	3/64 16A		25-2b/X	70.7	No	253AY	Derby
5256	25.106	3/64 16A		25-2b/X	70.7	No	253AY	Derby
5257	25.107	3/64 16A	5/81 TO	25-2b/X	70.7	No	253AY	Derby
5258	25.108	3/64 16A	7/80 ED	25-2b/X	70.7	No	253AY	Derby
5259	25.109	3/64 16A		25-2b/X	70.7	No	253AY	Derby
5260	25.110	3/64 16A	11/80 SP	25-2b/X	70.7	No	253AY	Derby
5261	25.111	4/64 16A	3/80 CW	25-2b/X	70.7	No	253AY	Derby
5262	25.112	4/64 16A	11/80 CW	25-2b/X	70.7	No	253AY	Derby
5263	25.113	4/64 16A		25-2b/X	70.7	No	253AY	Derby
5264	25.114	4/64 16A	2/81 CW	25-2b/X	70.7	No	253AY	Derby
5265	25.115	4/64 16A		25-2b/X	70.7	No	253AY	Derby
5266	25.116	4/64 16A	11/80 CW	25-2b/X	70.7	No	253AY	Derby
5267	25.117	5/64 16A		25-2b/X	70.7	No	253AY	Derby
5268	25.118	5/64 16A	1/81 TO	25-2b/V	70.7	No	253AY	Derby
5269	25.119	5/64 16A		25-2b/V	70.7	No	253AY	Derby
5270	25.120	5/64 16A		25-2b/X	70.7	No	253AY	Derby
5271	25.121	5/64 16A	11/80 TO	25-2b/X	70.7	No	253AY	Derby
5272	25.122	5/64 16A	11/80 TO	25-2b/X	70.7	No	253AY	Derby
5273	25.123	6/64 16A		25-2b/X	70.7	No	253AY	Derby
5274	25.124	6/64 16A		25-2b/X	70.7	No	253AY	Derby
5275	25.125	6/64 16A		25-2b/X	70.7	No	253AY	Derby
5276	25.126	6/64 16A		25-2b/X	70.7	No	253AY	Derby
5277	25.127	6/64 16A	11/80 TO	25-2b/X	70.7	No	253AY	Derby
5278		6/64 16A	5/71 TO	25-2b/X	70.7	No	253AY	Derby
5279	25.129	6/64 16A	2/82 TO	25-2b/X	70.7	No	253AY	Derby
5280	25.130	6/64 16A		25-2b/X	70.7	No	253AY	Derby
5281	25.131	6/64 16A		25-2b/X	70.7	No	253AY	Derby
5282	25.132	6/64 16A		25-2b/X	70.7	No	253AY	Derby
5283	25.133	7/64 16A		25-2b/X	70.7	No	253AY	Derby
5284	25.134	7/64 16A		25-2b/X	70.7	No	253AY	Derby
5285	25.135	7/64 16A		25-2b/X	70.7	No	253AY	Derby
5286	25.136	7/64 16A		25-2b/X	70.7	No	253AY	Derby
5287	25.137	7/64 16A	11/80 TO	25-2b/X	70.7	No	253AY	Derby
5288	25.138	8/64 16A		25-2b/X	70.7	No	253AY	Derby
5289	25.139	8/64 16A		25-2b/X	70.7	No	253AY	Derby
5290	25.140	8/64 16A		25-2b/X	70.7	No	253AY	Derby
5291	25.141	8/64 16A		25-2b/X	70.7	No	253AY	Derby
5292	25.142	9/64 16A	7/81 KD	25-2b/X	70.7	No	253AY	Derby
5293	25.143	9/64 16A		25-2b/X	70.7	No	253AY	Derby
5294	25.144	9/64 16A		25-2b/X	70.7	No	253AY	Derby
5295	25.145	9/64 16A		25-2b/X	70.7	No	253AY	Derby
5296	25.146	9/64 16A		25-2b/X	70.7	No	253AY	Derby
5297	25.147	9/64 16A	3/80 KD	25-2b/X	70.7	No	253AY	Derby
5298	25.148	9/64 16A		25-2b/X	70.7	No	253AY	Derby
5299	25.149	10/64 16A	1/82 KD	25-2b/X	70.7	No	253AY	Derby
7500	25.150	10/64 16A		25-2b/X	70.7	No	253AY	Derby
7501	25.151	10/64 16A		25-2b/X	70.7	No	253AY	Derby
7502	25.152	10/64 16A		25-2b/X	70.7	No	253AY	Derby
7503	25.153	10/64 16A		25-2b/X	70.7	No	253AY	Derby
7504	25.154	10/64 16A		25-2b/X	70.7	No	253AY	Derby
7505	25.155	10/64 16A	12/80 LA/ZL	25-2b/X	70.7	No	253AY	Derby
7506	25.156	10/64 16A	12/80 CD	25-2b/X	70.7	No	253AY	Derby
7507	25.157	10/64 16A		25-2b/X	70.7	No	253AY	Derby
7508	25.158	11/64 16A		25-2b/V	70.7	No	253AY	Derby
7509	25.159	11/64 16A	11/80 CD	2000/11	70.7	No	253AY	Derby
7510	25.160	11/64 16A		2000/11	70.7	No	253AY	Derby
7511	25.161	11/64 16A		2000/11	70.7	No	253AY	Derby
7512	25.162	11/64 16A	5/81 CD	2000/11	70.7	No	253AY	Derby
7513	25.163	11/64 16A	11/80 CD	2000/11	70.7	No	253AY	Derby
7514	25.164	11/64 16A		2000/11	70.7	No	253AY	Derby
7515	25.165	11/64 16A	11/78 CD	2000/11	70.7	No	253AY	Derby
7516	25.166	12/64 16A	11/80 CD	2000/11	70.7	No	253AY	Derby
7517	25.167	12/64 16A		25-2c/X	70.7	No	253AY	Derby
7518	25.168	12/64 16A		25-2c/X	70.7	No	253AY	Derby
7519	25.169	1/65 M16	9/81 CD	25-2c/X	70.7	No	253AY	Derby
7520	25.120	12/64 16A	4/82 CD	25-2c/X	70.7	No	253AY	Derby
7521	25.171	1/65 M16	10/78 HA	25-2c/X	70.7	No	253AY	Derby
7522	25.172	1/65 M16	2/81 SP	25-2c/X	70.7	No	253AY	Derby
7523	25.173	1/65 M16		25-2c/X	74.4	No	253AY	Derby
7524	25.174	1/65 M16	9/76 CW	25-2c/X	74.4	No	253AY	Derby
7525	25.175	1/65 M16		25-2e/X	70.6	No	253AY	Derby
7526	25.176	1/65 M16		25-2e/X	70.6	No	253AY	Derby

Orig No	TOPS No	To Stock	Withdrawn	Diagram	Weight (T)	Boiler	Tr Motor Type	Builder
7527	25.177	1/65 M16		25-2e/X	70.6	No	253AY	Derby
7528	25.178	1/65 M16		25-2e/X	70.6	No	253AY	Derby
7529	25.179	2/65 M16		25-2e/X	70.6	No	253AY	Derby
7530	25.180	2/65 M16		25-2e/X	70.6	No	253AY	Derby
7531	25.181	2/65 M16		25-2e/X	70.6	No	253AY	Derby
7532	25.182	2/65 M16		25-2e/X	70.6	No	253AY	Derby
7533	25.183	2/65 M16	12/80 CW/ZL	25-2e/X	70.6	No	253AY	Derby
7534	25.184	3/65 M16		25-2e/X	70.6	No	253AY	Derby
7535	25.185	3/65 M16		25-2e/X	70.6	No	253AY	Derby
7536	25.186	3/65 M16		25-2e/X	70.6	No	253AY	Derby
7537	25.187	3/66 M16		25-2e/X	70.6	No	253AY	Derby
7538	25.188	3/65 M16		25-2e/X	70.6	No	253AY	Derby
7539	25.189	3/65 M16		25-2e/X	70.6	No	253AY	Derby
7540	25.190	4/65 M16		25-2e/X	70.6	No	253AY	Derby
7541	25.191	4/65 M16		25-2e/X	70.6	No	253AY	Derby
7542	25.192	4/65 M16		25-2e/X	70.6	No	253AY	Derby
7543	25.193	4/65 M16		25-2e/X	70.6	No	253AY	Derby
7544	25.194	5/65 M16		25-2e/X	70.6	No	253AY	Derby
7545	25.195	5/65 M16		25-2e/X	70.6	No	253AY	Derby
7546	25.196	5/65 M16		25-2e/X	70.6	No	253AY	Derby
7547	25.197	5/65 M16	12/80 BS/ZL	25-2e/X	70.6	No	253AY	Derby
7548	25.198	5/65 M16		25-2e/X	70.6	No	253AY	Derby
7549	25.199	5/65 M16		25-2e/X	70.6	No	253AY	Derby
7550	25.200	6/65 M16		25-2e/X	70.6	No	253AY	Derby
7551	25.201	6/65 M16		25-2e/X	70.6	No	253AY	Derby
7552	25.202	6/65 M16		25-2e/X	70.6	No	253AY	Derby
7553	25.203	6/65 ML	12/80 CW/ZL	25-2e/X	70.6	No	253AY	Derby
7554	25.204	6/65 ML	7/80 CW	25-2e/X	70.6	No	253AY	Derby
7555	25.205	7/65 M16		25-2e/X	70.6	No	253AY	Derby
7556	25.206	7/65 M16		25-2e/X	70.6	No	253AY	Derby
7557	25.207	8/65 M16		25-2e/X	70.6	No	253AY	Derby
7558	25.208	9/65 M16		25-2e/X	70.6	No	253AY	Derby
7559	25.209	8/65 M16		25-2e/X	70.6	No	253AY	Derby
7560	25.210	9/65 M16		25-2e/X	70.6	No	253AY	Derby
7561	25.211	10/65 M16		25-2e/X	70.6	No	253AY	Derby
7562	25.212	11/65 M16		25-2e/X	70.6	No	253AY	Derby
7563	25.213	11/65 M16		25-2e/X	70.6	No	253AY	Derby
7564	25.214	12/65 M16		25-2e/X	70.6	No	253AY	Derby
7565	25.215	1/66 M16		25-2e/X	70.6	No	253AY	Derby
7566	25.216	1/66 M16	12/80 CD	25-2e/X	70.6	No	253AY	Derby
7567	25.217	1/66 M16	2/81 CD	25-2e/X	70.6	No	253AY	Derby
7568	25.218	19/63 18A		25-1a/X	74.4	Yes	253AY	Derby
7569	25.219	10/63 14A		25-2d/V	73.75	Yes	253AY	Derby
7570	25.220	10/63 18A		25-2d/V	73.75	Yes	253AY	Derby
7571	25.221	10/63 14A		25-1c/X	74.4	Yes	253AY	Derby
7572	25.222	10/63 14A	12/80 LO	25-1c/X	74.4	Yes	253AY	Derby
7573	25.223	10/63 14A	10/80 LA	25-2d/V	73.75	Yes	253AY	Derby
7574	25.224	11/63 14A		25-2d/V	73.75	Yes	253AY	Derby
7575	25.225	11/63 16A	10/80 LA	25-2d/V	73.75	Yes	253AY	Derby
7576	25.226	11/63 16A		25-2d/V	73.75	Yes	253AY	Derby
7577	25.227	11/63 16A		25-2c/X	74.4	Yes	253AY	Derby
7578	25.228	12/63 16A		25-2d/V	73.75	Yes	253AY	Darlington
7579	25.229	12/63 16A		25-2d/V	73.75	Yes	253AY	Darlington
7580	25.230	12/63 16A		25-1c/X	74.4	Yes	253AY	Darlington
7581	25.231	1/64 16A		2000/8	73.75	Yes	253AY	Darlington
7582	25.232	1/64 16A	12/80 ED	25-1c/X	74.4	Yes	253AY	Darlington
7583	25.233	1/64 16A		25-1c/X	74.4	Yes	253AY	Darlington
7584	25.234	1/64 16A		25-1c/X	74.4	Yes	253AY	Darlington
7585	25.235	1/64 16A		25-2c/X	74.4	Yes	253AY	Darlington
7586	25.236	2/64 16A		25-1c/X	74.4	Yes	253AY	Darlington
7587	25.237	2/64 16A		25-1c/X	74.4	Yes	253AY	Darlington
7588	25.238	3/64 16A	10/80 ED	25-1c/X	74.4	Yes	253AY	Darlington
7589	25.239	4/64 16A		25-1c/X	74.4	Yes	253AY	Darlington
7590	25.240	4/64 16A		25-1c/X	74.4	Yes	253AY	Darlington
7591	25.241	4/64 16A	5/81 ED	25-1c/X	74.4	Yes	253AY	Darlington
7592	25.242	5/64 16A		25-2d/X	73.75	Yes	253AY	Darlington
7593	25.243	5/64 16A		25-1c/X	74.4	Yes	253AY	Darlington
7594	25.244	6/64 16A		25-2d/V	73.75	Yes	253AY	Darlington
7595	25.245	6/64 16A		25-2d/V	73.75	Yes	253AY	Darlington
7596	25.246	7/64 16A		25-1c/X	74.4	Yes	253AY	Darlington
7597	25.247	8/64 16A		25-2d/X	73.75	Yes	253AY	Darlington
7598	25.248	2/66 41A		25-3a/X	70.7	No	253AY	Derby
7599	25.249	2/66 41A		25-3a/X	70.6	No	253AY	Derby

Orig No	TOPS No	To Stock	Withdrawn	Diagram	Weight (T)	Boiler	Tr Motor Type	Builder
7600	25.250	2/66 41A		25-3a/X	70.6	No	253AY	Derby
7601	25.251	2/66 41A		25-3a/X	70.6	No	253AY	Derby
7602	25.252	2/66 41A	3/80 BS	25-3a/X	70.6	No	253AY	Derby
7603	25.253	2/66 41A		25-3a/X	70.6	No	253AY	Derby
7604	25.254	3/66 41A		25-3b/X	70.6	No	253AY	Derby
7605	25.255	3/66 41A		25-3b/X	70.6	No	253AY	Derby
7606	25.256	3/66 41A		25-3b/X	70.6	No	253AY	Derby
7607	25.257	3/66 41A		25-3b/X	70.6	No	253AY	Derby
7608	25.258	4/66 41A		25-3b/X	70.6	No	253AY	Derby
7609	25.259	4/66 41A		25-3b/X	70.6	No	253AY	Derby
7610	25.260	4/66 41A		25-3b/X	70.6	No	253AY	Derby
7611	25.261	4/66 65A	1/81 BS	25-3b/X	70.6	No	253AY	Derby
7612	25.262	4/66 65A		25-3b/X	70.6	No	253AY	Derby
7613	25.263	4/66 65A	11/80 BS	25-3b/X	70.6	No	253AY	Derby
7614	25.264	5/66 65A	12/80 TO	25-3b/X	70.6	No	253AY	Derby
7615	25.265	5/66 65A		25-3b/X	70.6	No	253AY	Derby
7616	25.266	5/66 65A		25-3b/X	70.6	No	253AY	Derby
7617	25.267	7/66 65A	2/81 TO	25-3b/X	70.6	No	253AY	Derby
7618	25.268	8/66 65A		25-3b/X	70.6	No	253AY	Derby
7619	25.269	8/66 65A		25-3b/X	70.6	No	253AY	Derby
7620	25.270	8/66 65A		25-3b/X	70.6	No	253AY	Derby
7621	25.271	9/66 65A	7/81 BS	25-3b/X	70.6	No	253AY	Derby
7622	25.272	10/66 65A	7/81 BS	25-3b/X	70.6	No	253AY	Derby
7623	25.273	10/66 65A	2/81 BS	25-3b/X	70.6	No	253AY	Derby
7624	25.274	7/65 41A		25-3b/V	70.7	No	253AY	B-P
7625	25.275	7/65 41A	4/82 BS	25-3a/V	70.7	No	253AY	B-P
7626	25.276	8/65 41A		25-3a/V	70.7	No	253AY	B-P
7627	25.277	8/65 41A		25-3b/X	70.6	No	253AY	B-P
7628	25.278	8/65 41A		25-3b/X	70.6	No	253AY	B-P
7629	25.279	9/65 41A		25-3b/X	70.6	No	253AY	B-P
7630	25.280	9/65 41A	11/81 TO	25-3b/X	70.6	No	253AY	B-P
7631	25.281	9/65 41A	2/81 SP	25-3b/X	70.6	No	253AY	B-P
7632	25.282	10/65 41A		25-3b/X	70.6	No	253AY	B-P
7633	25.283	10/65 41A		25-3b/X	70.6	No	253AY	B-P
7634	25.284	10/65 41A		25-3b/X	70.6	No	253AY	B-P
7635	25.285	11/65 41A		25-3b/X	70.6	No	253AY	B-P
7636	25.286	11/65 41A		25-3b/X	70.6	No	253AY	B-P
7637	25.287	11/65 41A		25-3b/X	70.6	No	253AY	B-P
7638	25.288	11/65 41A		25-3b/X	70.6	No	253AY	B-P
7639	25.289	12/65 41A		25-3b/X	70.6	No	253AY	B-P
7640	25.290	12/65 41A	7/81 CD	25-3b/X	70.6	No	253AY	B-P
7641	25.291	1/66 41A	5/81 CD	25-3b/X	70.6	No	253AY	B-P
7642	25.292	1/66 41A	7/81 CD	25-3b/X	70.6	No	253AY	B-P
7643	25.293	2/66 41A	2/81 CD	25-3b/X	70.6	No	253AY	B-P
7644	25.294	2/66 41A		25-3b/X	70.6	No	253AY	B-P
7645	25.295	3/66 41A	6/78 CW	25-3b/X	70.6	No	253AY	B-P
7646	25.296	3/66 41A		25-3b/X	70.6	No	253AY	B-P
7647	25.297	4/66 41A		25-3b/X	70.6	No	253AY	B-P
7648	25.298	4/66 41A		25-3b/X	70.6	No	253AY	B-P
7649	25.299	4/66 41A	7/81 CW	25-3b/X	70.6	No	253AY	B-P
7650	25.300	5/66 D16		25-3b/X	70.6	No	253AY	B-P
7651	25.301	5/66 D16		25-3b/X	70.6	No	253AY	B-P
7652	25.302	5/66 D16		25-3b/X	70.6	No	253AY	B-P
7653	25.303	6/66 ML		25-3b/X	70.6	No	253AY	B-P
7654	25.304	6/66 ML		25-3b/X	70.6	No	253AY	B-P
7655	25.305	6/66 ML		25-3b/X	70.6	No	253AY	B-P
7656	25.306	7/66 ML		25-3b/X	70.6	No	253AY	B-P
7657	25.307	7/66 ML		25-3b/X	70.6	No	253AY	B-P
7658	25.308	7/66 ML		25-3b/X	70.6	No	253AY	B-P
7659	25.309	7/66 ML		25-3b/X	70.6	No	253AY	B-P
7660	25.310	12/66 D01		25-3b/X	70.6	No	253AY	Derby
7661	25.311	11/66 D01		25-3b/X	70.6	No	253AY	Derby
7662	25.312	11/66 D01		25-3b/X	70.6	No	253AY	Derby
7663	25.313	11/66 D01		25-3b/X	70.6	No	253AY	Derby
7664	25.314	11/66 D01		25-3b/X	70.6	No	253AY	Derby
7665	25.315	12/66 D01		25-3b/X	70.6	No	253AY	Derby
7666	25.316	12/66 D01		25-3b/X	70.6	No	253AY	Derby
7667	25.317	1/67 D01		25-3b/X	70.6	No	253AY	Derby
7668	25.318	1/67 D01		25-3b/X	70.6	No	253AY	Derby
7669	25.319	3/67 D01		25-3b/X	70.6	No	253AY	Derby
7670	25.320	1/67 D01		25-3b/X	70.6	No	253AY	Derby
7671	25.321	2/67 D01		25-3b/X	70.6	No	253AY	Derby
7672	25.322	2/67 D16		25-3b/X	70.6	No	253AY	Derby

Orig No	TOPS No	To Stock	Withdrawn	Diagram	Weight (T)	Boiler	Tr Motor Type	Builder
7673	25.323	3/67 D16		25-3b/X	70.6	No	253AY	Derby
7674	25.324	3/67 D16		25-3b/X	70.6	No	253AY	Derby
7675	25.325	4/67 D16		25-3b/X	70.6	No	253AY	Derby
7676	25.326	4/67 D16		25-3b/X	70.6	No	253AY	Derby
7677	25.327	5/67 D16		25-3b/X	70.6	No	253AY	Derby

ZL = Swindon stored

Class 26/27

Orig No	TOPS No	To Stock	Withdrawn	Diagram	Weight (T)	Boiler	Builder	No/Date
5300	26.007	8/58 34B		26-a/X	73.85	No	BRCW	45-1958
5301	26.001	9/58 34B		26-a/X	73.85	No	BRCW	46-1958
5302	26.002	10/58 34B		26-a/X	73.85	No	BRCW	47-1958
5303	26.003	10/58 34B*		25-a/X	73.85	No	BRCW	48-1958
5304	26.004	10/58 34B		26-a/X	73.85	No	BRCW	49-1958
5305	26.005	11/58 34B		26-a/X	73.85	No	BRCW	50-1958
5306	26.006	11/58 34B		26-a/X	73.85	No	BRCW	51-1958
5307	26.020	12/58 34B	2/77 IS	26-b/V	77.85	Yes	BRCW	52-1958
5308	26.008	12/58 34B		26-b/V	77.85	Yes	BRCW	53-1958
5309	26.009	12/58 34B	1/77 IS	26-b/V	77.85	Yes	BRCW	54-1958
5310	26.010	1/59 34B		26-b/V	77.85	Yes	BRCW	55-1958
5311	26.011	1/59 34B		26-b/V	77.85	Yes	BRCW	56-1958
5312	26.012	1/59 34B	2/82 HA	26-b/V	77.85	Yes	BRCW	57-1958
5313	26.013	1/59 34B		26-b/V	77.85	Yes	BRCW	58-1958
5314	26.014	2/59 34B		26-b/V	77.85	Yes	BRCW	59-1958
5315	26.015	2/59 34B		26-b/V	77.85	Yes	BRCW	60-1958
5316	26.016	2/59 34B	10/75 HA	26-b/V	77.85	Yes	BRCW	61-1958
5317	26.017	2/59 34B	8/77 ED	26-b/V	77.85	Yes	BRCW	62-1958
5318	26.018	3/59 34B	2/82 HA	26-b/V	77.85	Yes	BRCW	63-1958
5319	26.019	3/59 34B		26-b/V	77.85	Yes	BRCW	64-1958
5320	26.028	4/59 64B		26-1a/V	73.3	Yes	BRCW	65-1958
5321	26.021	4/59 64B		26-1a/V	73.3	Yes	BRCW	66-1958
5322	26.022	4/59 64B	2/81 HA	26-1a/V	73.3	Yes	BRCW	67-1958
5323	26.023	5/59 64B		26-1a/V	73.3	Yes	BRCW	68-1958
5324	26.024	5/59 64B		26-1a/V	73.3	Yes	BRCW	69-1958
5325	26.025	5/59 64B		26-1a/V	73.3	Yes	BRCW	70-1958
5326	26.026	5/59 64B		26-1a/V	73.3	Yes	BRCW	71-1958
5327	26.027	6/59 64B		26-1a/V	73.3	Yes	BRCW	72-1958
5328		6/59 64B	7/72 64B	26-1a/V	73.3	Yes	BRCW	73-1958
5329	26.029	6/59 64B		26-1a/V	73.3	Yes	BRCW	74-1958
5330	26.030	6/59 64B		26-1a/V	73.3	Yes	BRCW	75-1958
5331	26.031	6/59 64B		26-1a/V	73.3	Yes	BRCW	76-1958
5332	26.032	7/59 64B		26-1a/V	73.3	Yes	BRCW	77-1958
5333	26.033	7/59 64B		26-1a/V	73.3	Yes	BRCW	78-1958
5334	26.034	7/59 64B		26-1a/V	73.3	Yes	BRCW	79-1958
5335	26.035	7/59 64B		26-1a/V	73.3	Yes	BRCW	80-1958
5336	26.036	8/59 64B		26-1a/V	73.3	Yes	BRCW	81-1958
5337	26.037	8/59 64B		26-1a/V	73.3	Yes	BRCW	82-1958
5338	26.038	8/59 64B		26-1a/V	73.3	Yes	BRCW	83-1959
5339	26.039	9/59 64B		26-1a/V	73.3	Yes	BRCW	84-1959
5340	26.040	9/59 64B		26-1a/V	73.3	Yes	BRCW	85-1959
5341	26.041	9/59 64B		26-1a/V	73.3	Yes	BRCW	86-1959
5342	26.042	9/59 64B		26-1a/V	73.3	Yes	BRCW	87-1959
5343	26.043	10/59 60A		26-1a/V	73.3	Yes	BRCW	88-1959
5344	26.044	10/59 60A		26-1a/V	73.3	Yes	BRCW	89-1959
5345	26.045	10/59 64B		26-1a/V	73.3	Yes	BRCW	90-1959
5346	26.046	10/59 64B		26-1a/V	73.3	Yes	BRCW	91-1959
5347	27.001	6/61 62A		27-a/V	73.3	Yes	BRCW	190-1961
5348	27.002	7/61 62A		27-a/V	73.3	Yes	BRCW	191-1961
5349	27.003	7/61 65A		27-a/V	73.3	Yes	BRCW	192-1961
5350	27.004	8/61 65A		27-a/V	73.3	Yes	BRCW	193-1961
5351	27.005	8/61 65A		27-a/V	73.3	Yes	BRCW	194-1961
5352	27.006	9/61 65A	1/76 ED	27-a/V	73.3	Yes	BRCW	195-1961
5353	27.007	9/61 65A		27-a/V	73.3	Yes	BRCW	196-1961
5354	27.008	9/61 65A		27-a/V	73.3	Yes	BRCW	197-1961

Orig No	TOPS No	To Stock	Withdrawn	Diagram	Weight (T)	Boiler	Builder	No/Date
5355	27.009	9/61 65A	7/80 ED	27-a/V	73.3	Yes	BRCW	198-1961
5356	27.010	10/61 65A		27-a/V	73.3	Yes	BRCW	199-1961
5357	27.011	10/61 65A	3/81 ED	27-a/V	72.3	Yes	BRCW	200-1961
5358	27.012	10/61 65A		27-a/V	73.3	Yes	BRCW	201-1961
5359	27.013	11/61 65A	7/76 ED	27-a/V	73.3	Yes	BRCW	202-1961
5360	27.014	11/61 65A		27-a/V	73.3	Yes	BRCW	203-1961
5361	27.015	11/61 65A	1/77 ED	27-a/V	73.3	Yes	BRCW	204-1961
5362	27.016	11/61 65A		27-a/V	73.3	Yes	BRCW	205-1961
5363	27.017	12/61 65A		27-a/V	73.3	Yes	BRCW	206-1961
5364	27.018	12/61 65A		27-a/V	73.3	Yes	BRCW	207-1961
5365	27.019	12/61 65A		27-a/V	73.3	Yes	BRCW	208-1961
5366	27.020	12/61 65A		27-a/V	73.3	Yes	BRCW	209-1961
5367	27.021	12/61 65A		27-a/V	73.3	Yes	BRCW	210-1961
5368	27.022	12/61 65A		27-a/V	73.3	Yes	BRCW	211-1961
5369	27.023	12/61 65A		27-a/V	73.3	Yes	BRCW	212-1961
5370	27.024	1/62 51L		27-b/V	71.2	No	BRCW	213-1961
5371	27.025	1/62 51L		27-b/V	71.2	No	BRCW	214-1961
5372	27.026	1/62 51L		27-b/V	71.2	No	BRCW	215-1961
5373	27.027	1/62 51L		27-b/V	71.2	No	BRCW	216-1961
5374	27.101	2/62 51L		27-1b/X	75.74	No	BRCW	217-1961
5375	27.028	2/62 51L		27-b/V	71.2	No	BRCW	218-1961
5376	27.029	2/62 51L		27-b/V	71.2	No	BRCW	219-1961
5377	27.030	2/62 51L		27-b/V	71.2	No	BRCW	220
5378	27.031	3/62 51L	5/78 ED	27-b/V	71.2	No	BRCW	221
5379	27.032	3/62 14A		27-b/V	71.2	No	BRCW	222
5380	27.102	3/62 14A		27-1b/X	73.45	No	BRCW	225
5381	27.033	4/62 14A		27-b/V	71.2	No	BRCW	224
5382	27.034	4/62 14A		27-b/V	71.2	No	BRCW	225
5383		4/62 14A		27-b/V	71.2	No	BRCW	226
5384	27.035	5/62 14A	9/76 ED	27-b/V	71.2	Yes	BRCW	227
5385	27.036	5/62 14A		27-b/V	71.2	No	BRCW	228
5386	27.103	5/62 14A		27-1b/X	75.45	No	BRCW	229
5387	27.104	5/62 14A		27-1b/X	75.45	No	BRCW	230
5388	27.105	5/62 14A		27-1b/X	75.45	No	BRCW	231
5389	27.037	6/62 14A		27-b/V	71.2	No	BRCW	232
5390	27.038	6/62 14A		27-c/X	76.4	No	BRCW	233
5391	27.201 27.119	6/62 14A	1/79 HA	17-2a/X	75.55	No	BRCW	234
5392	27.202 27.120	6/62 14A	8/80 ED	27-2a/X	75.55	No	BRCW	235
5393	27.203 27.121	6/62 14A		27-2a/X	75.55	No	BRCW	236
5394	27.106	6/62 14A		27-1b/X	75.45	No	BRCW	237
5395	27.107	7/62 14A		27-1b/X	75.45	No	BRCW	238
5396	27.108	7/62 14A		27-1b/X	75.45	No	BRCW	239
5397	27.109	7/62 14A		27-1b/X	75.45	No	BRCW	240
5398	27.039	7/62 14A	10/75 ED	27-b/V	71.2	No	BRCW	241
5399	27.110	7/62 14A		27-1b/X	75.45	No	BRCW	242
5400	27.111	7/62 14A		27-1B/X	75.45	No	BRCW	245
5401	27.112	7/62 14A		27-1b/X	75.45	No	BRCW	244
5402	27.040	7/62 14A		27-b/V	71.2	No	BRCW	245
5403	27.204 27.122	7/62 14A		27-2a/X	75.55	No	BRCW	246
5404	27.205 27.113	7/62 14A		27-2a/X	75.55	No	BRCW	247
5405	27.041	7/62 14A		27-d/X	76.2	Yes	BRCW	248
5406	27.042	8/62 14A		27-b/V	71.2	No	BRCW	249
5407	27.206 27.114	8/62 14A		27-2a/X	75.55	No	BRCW	250
5408	27.207 27.115	8/62 14A		27-2a/X	75.55	No	BRCW	251
5409	27.208 27.116	8/62 14A		27-2a/X	75.55	No	BRCW	22
5410	27.209 27.123	8/62 14A		27-2a/X	75.55	No	BRCW	253
5411	27.210 27.117	8/62 14A		27-2a/X	75.55	No	BRCW	24
5412	27.211 27.124	8/62 14A		27-2a/X	75.55	No	BRCW	255
5413	27.212 27.118	9/62 14A		27-2a/X	75.55	No	BRCW	256
5414	27.043	9/62 14A	4/80 ED	27-b/V	71.2	No	BRCW	257
5415	27.044	9/62 14A	7/80 ED	27-b/V	71.2	No	BRCW	258

* ScR

Class 33

Orig No	TOPS No	To Stock	Withdrawn	Diagram	Weight (T)	Builder	No/Date
6500	33.001	1/60 73C		3002/1	73.4	BRCW	92-1959
6501	33.002	2/60 73C		3002/1	73.4	BRCW	93-1959
6502	—	3/60 73C	3/64 73C	3002/1	73.4	BRCW	94-1960
6503	33.003	3/60 73C		3002/1	73.4	BRCW	95-1960
6504	33.004	3/60 73C		3002/1	73.4	BRCW	96-1960
6505	33.005	4/60 73C		3002/1	73.4	BRCW	97-1960
6506	33.006	4/60 73C		3002/1	73.4	BRCW	98-1960
6507	33.007	5/60 73C		3002/1	73.4	BRCW	99-1960
6508	33.008	5/60 73C		3002/1	73.4	BRCW	100-1960
6509	33.009	5/60 73C		3002/1	73.4	BRCW	101-1960
6510	33.010	6/60 73C		3002/1	73.4	BRCW	102-1960
6511	33.101	6/60 73C		3002/3	77.3	BRCW	103-1960
6512	33.011	6/60 73C		3002/1	73.4	BRCW	104-1960
6513	33.102	6/60 73C		3002/3	77.3	BRCW	105-1960
6514	33.103	7/60 73C		3002/3	77.3	BRCW	106-1960
6515	33.012	7/60 73C		3002/1	73.4	BRCW	107-1960
6516	33.104	7/60 73C		3002/3	77.3	BRCW	108-1960
6517	33.105	7/60 73C		3002/3	77.3	BRCW	109-1960
6518	33.013	8/60 73C		3002/1	73.4	BRCW	110-1960
6519	33.106	8/60 73C		3002/3	77.3	BRCW	111-1960
6520	33.107	9/60 73C		3002/3	77.3	BRCW	112-1960
6521	33.108	9/60 73C		3002/3	77.3	BRCW	113-1960
6522	33.014	9/60 73C		3002/1	73.4	BRCW	114-1960
6523	33.015	9/60 73C		3002/1	73.4	BRCW	115-1960
6524	33.016	10/60 73C		3002/1	73.4	BRCW	116-1960
6525	33.109	10/60 73C		3002/3	77.3	BRCW	117-1960

No 33.016 passes Crewe Bank, just north of Shrewsbury on 13 March 1983 with the 07.50 Cardiff-Crewe. *Bill Chapman*

Orig No	TOPS No	To Stock	Withdrawn	Diagram	Weight (T)	Builder	No/Date
6526	33.017	10/60 73C		3002/1	73.4	BRCW	118-1960
6527	33.110	10/60 73C		3002/3	77.3	BRCW	119-1960
6528	33.111	10/60 73C		3002/3	77.3	BRCW	120-1960
6529	33.112	11/60 73C		3002/3	77.3	BRCW	121-1960
6530	33.018	11/60 73C		3002/1	73.4	BRCW	122-1960
6531	33.113	11/60 73C		3002/3	77.3	BRCW	123-1960
6532	33.114	11/60 73C		3002/3	77.3	BRCW	124-1960
6533	33.115	12/60 73C		3002/3	77.3	BRCW	125-1960
6534	33.019	12/60 73C		3002/1	73.4	BRCW	126-1960
6535	33.116	12/60 73C		3002/3	77.3	BRCW	127-1960
6536	33.117	12/60 73C		3002/3	77.3	BRCW	128-1960
6537	33.020	12/60 73C		3002/1	73.4	BRCW	129-1960
6538	33.118	1/61 73C		3002/3	77.3	BRCW	130-1960
6539	33.021	1/61 73C		3002/1	73.4	BRCW	131-1960
6540	33.022	1/61 73C		3002/1	73.4	BRCW	132-1960
6541	33.023	1/61 73C		3002/1	73.4	BRCW	133-1960
6542	33.024	2/61 73C		3002/1	73.4	BRCW	134-1960
6543	33.025	2/61 73C		3002/1	73.4	BRCW	135-1960
6544	33.026	2/61 73C		3002/1	73.4	BRCW	136-1961
6545	33.027	3/61 73C		3002/1	73.4	BRCW	137-1961
6546	33.028	3/61 73C		3002/1	73.4	BRCW	138-1961
6547	33.029	3/61 73C		3002/1	73.4	BRCW	139-1961
6548	33.030	4/61 73C		3002/1	73.4	BRCW	140-1961
6549	33.031	4/61 73C		3002/1	73.4	BRCW	141-1961
6550	33.032	4/61 73C		3002/1	73.4	BRCW	142-1961
6551	33.033	4/61 73C		3002/1	73.4	BRCW	143-1961
6552	33.034	4/61 73C		3002/1	73.4	BRCW	144-1961
6553	33.035	5/61 73C		3002/1	73.4	BRCW	145-1961
6554	33.036	5/61 73C	7/79 HG	3002/1	73.4	BRCW	146-1961
6555	33.037	5/61 73C		3002/1	73.4	BRCW	147-1961
6556	33.038	6/61 73C		3002/1	73.4	BRCW	148-1961
6557	33.039	6/61 73C		3002/1	73.4	BRCW	149-1961
6558	33.040	6/61 73C		3002/1	73.4	BRCW	150-1961
6559	33.041	6/61 73C	11/75 HG	3002/1	73.4	BRCW	151-1961
6560	33.042	7/61 73C		3002/1	73.4	BRCW	152-1961
6561	33.043	7/61 73C		3002/1	73.4	BRCW	153-1961
6562	33.044	7/61 73C		3002/1	73.4	BRCW	154-1961
6563	33.045	7/61 73C		3002/1	73.4	BRCW	155-1961
6564	33.046	7/61 73C		3002/1	73.4	BRCW	156-1961
6565	33.047	8/61 73C		3002/1	73.4	BRCW	169-1961
6566	33.048	8/61 73C		3002/1	73.4	BRCW	170-1961
6567	33.049	9/61 73C		3002/1	73.4	BRCW	171-1961
6568	33.050	9/61 73C		3002/1	73.4	BRCW	172-1961
6569	33.051	9/61 73C		3002/1	73.4	BRCW	173-1961
6570	33.052	9/61 73C		3002/1	73.4	BRCW	174-1961
6571	33.053	10/61 73C		3002/1	73.4	BRCW	175-1961
6572	33.054	10/61 73C		3002/1	73.4	BRCW	176-1961
6573	33.055	11/61 73C		3002/1	73.4	BRCW	177-1961
6574	33.056	10/61 73C		3002/1	73.4	BRCW	178-1961
6575	33.057	11/61 73C		3002/1	73.4	BRCW	179-1961
6576		11/61 73C	11/68 73C	3002/1	73.4	BRCW	180-1961
6577	33.058	11/61 73C		3002/1	73.4	BRCW	181-1961
6578	33.059	11/61 73C		3002/1	73.4	BRCW	182-1961
6579	33.060	12/61 73C		3002/1	73.4	BRCW	183-1961
6580	33.119	12/61 73C		3002/3	77.3	BRCW	184-1961
6581	33.061	12/61 73C		3002/1	73.4	BRCW	185-1961
6582	33.062	12/61 73C		3002/1	73.4	BRCW	186-1961
6583	33.063	1/62 73C		3002/1	73.4	BRCW	187-1961
6584	33.064	1/62 73C		3002/1	73.4	BRCW	188-1961
6585	33.065	1/62 73C		3002/1	73.4	BRCW	189-1961
6586	33.201	2/62 73C		3002/2	74.2	BRCW	157-1962
6587	33.202	2/62 73C		3002/2	74.2	BRCW	158-1962
6588	33.203	2/62 73C		3002/2	74.2	BRCW	159-1962
6589	33.204	2/62 73C		3002/2	74.2	BRCW	160-1962
6590	33.205	2/62 73C		3002/2	74.2	BRCW	161-1962
6591	33.206	3/62 73C		3002/2	74.2	BRCW	162-1962
6592	33.207	3/62 73C		3002/2	74.2	BRCW	163-1962
6593	33.208	3/62 73C		3002/2	74.2	BRCW	164-1962
6594	33.209	3/62 73C		3002/2	74.2	BRCW	165-1962
6595	33.210	4/62 73C		3002/2	74.2	BRCW	166-1962
6596	33.211	4/62 73C		3002/2	74.2	BRCW	167-1962
6597	33.212	5/62 73C		3002/2	74.2	BRCW	168-1962

Note: All ETH fitted